Creating a
Classroom
Newspaper

Kathleen Buss

Emeritus, University of Wisconsin—Stevens Point
Stevens Point, Wisconsin, USA

Leslie McClain-Ruelle

University of Wisconsin—Stevens Point
Stevens Point, Wisconsin, USA
Editors

INTERNATIONAL
Reading
Association

800 Barksdale Road, PO Box 8139
Newark, Delaware 19714-8139, USA
www.reading.org

The International Reading Association attempts, through its publications, to provide a forum for a wide spectrum of opinions on reading. This policy permits divergent viewpoints without implying the endorsement of the Association.

Director of Publications   Joan M. Irwin
Editorial Director, Books and Special Projects   Matthew W. Baker
Special Projects Editor   Tori Mello Bachman
Permissions Editor   Janet S. Parrack
Associate Editor   Jeanine K. McGann
Production Editor   Shannon Benner
Editorial Assistant   Pamela McComas
Publications Coordinator   Beth Doughty
Association Editor   David K. Roberts
Production Department Manager   Iona Sauscermen
Art Director   Boni Nash
Senior Electronic Publishing Specialist   Anette Schütz-Ruff
Electronic Publishing Specialist   Cheryl J. Strum
Electronic Publishing Assistant   John W. Cain

Project Editor   Tori Mello Bachman

Library of Congress Cataloging in Publication Data
Buss, Kathleen
   Creating a classroom newspaper/Kathleen Buss and Leslie McClain-Ruelle
     p.   cm.
   Includes bibliographical references.
   1. Student newspapers and periodicals. 2. Language arts (Elementary). 3. Education, Elementary—Activity programs.   I.McClain-Ruelle, Leslie II. Title.
LB3621.3 .M33   2000   00-040925
372.6—dc21
ISBN 0-87207-274-6

Dedication

To the Language Arts Block III students at the University of Wisconsin—Stevens Point, who are starting their careers as teachers.

Contents

Acknowledgments

W̲E̲ ̲W̲O̲U̲L̲D̲ like to thank the *Stevens Point Journal* for giving us a reason to write this book. Thank you Mark Larson, elementary education student at University of Wisconsin–Stevens Point, for designing this unit and helping with revisions. Thanks also to the 54 language arts students who contributed lessons.

We also would like to thank Betsy Wiberg and Sandy Davis, teachers of fourth grade at Plover–Whiting Elementary School in Plover, Wisconsin, who taught this unit and shared their students' work with us.

We would like to express our appreciation to the editors of the International Reading Association for their assistance. Thank you to Matthew Baker, Editorial Director of Books and Special Projects, for his suggestions that broadened the scope of this manuscript. Thanks also to Tori Mello Bachman, Special Projects Editor, for guiding this project with her knowledge of journalism.

Finally, thank you to the children who contributed their school newspapers and news articles, and thanks to the parents who gave us permission to use their children's work. A special note of thanks to Judy Anderson for her assistance in preparing this manuscript.

Introduction

THIS BOOK begins with an introduction to the newspaper and works through the concepts, vocabulary, and skills necessary to produce a publishable newspaper. Through the unit presented, students will develop a deeper understanding of themselves and others as members of a functioning society, and they will learn to be critically minded citizens who focus on public issues. Students will become involved in formulating questions and searching for answers. This book will help students in grades 3 through 6 integrate the knowledge from all disciplines—communication arts, science, social studies, fine arts, technology, and math—as they report about current events and about the lives of others in an unbiased and accurate way.

The unit Creating a Classroom Newspaper was developed when the Newspaper in Education staff of the *Stevens Point Journal* asked the School of Education at the University of Wisconsin–Stevens Point to create materials that could be used in the classroom to help students write articles for the newspaper. Mark Larson, an elementary education major with a background in journalism, outlined the concepts presented in this unit and prepared the Glossary of Newspaper Terms (Appendix E) as well as the Stylebook (Appendix F). Under the direction of Professor Kathleen Buss, the individual lessons were designed by 54 elementary education majors in the university's language arts methods classes. This unit was created to teach newspaper concepts, basic journalism, and how to write newspaper articles. The completed unit was so appealing that we have written this book to share the university students' unit with teachers of grades 3 through 6.

The unit was taught in classrooms across central Wisconsin

with the primary goal of creating a classroom newspaper for publication by a local newspaper. The student stories included in this book were collected from two fourth-grade classrooms. Two university preservice students who were involved in the development of this unit were placed in the classrooms for their university practicum experience. Other preservice students aided the classroom teacher and the practicum student with the teaching of this unit. The school newspapers and news articles that are shared in this book were created by students in these two fourth-grade classrooms. In celebration of Newspaper in Education Week, these classes' school newspapers were published in the *Stevens Point Journal*, a newspaper in rural Wisconsin.

Newspaper in Education

In order to understand the value of using newspaper activities in the classroom it is important to recognize the widespread use of these activities and the reading and writing skills they promote.

Using the newspaper in the classroom is not a new concept. Collaborative efforts between newspapers and schools date back to 1795. In early 1900, *The New York Times* initiated the first Newspaper in Education program (NIE) (Olivares, 1993). NIE is a cooperative venture in schools that uses newspapers to teach a variety of subjects (for example, history, reading, science, math, and composition) at all grade levels. NIE, since its inception in the 1930s, has become a far-reaching program that offers newspaper activities to use in the classroom for preschool through college level

students and beyond. There are currently over 700 NIE programs in place worldwide.

The purpose of the newspaper unit presented in this book is to offer strategies that are steeped in the communication arts (reading, writing, speaking, and listening), but most of the instructional strategies presented can be applied to the study of any curriculum area. The main concepts are modeled through teacher read alouds, teacher write alouds, authentic experiences with vocabulary, and the process of writing. After you model strategies and concepts, students will participate in reading and writing as they create a newspaper.

Most of the publications for using the newspaper in the classroom that have been published to date contain activities which use the newspaper to teach reading and content skills and strategies. The main emphasis has been on *reading* the newspaper. This unit focuses on actual student writing of a newspaper, and incorporates all the language arts processes. Throughout the lessons, the connections between these processes will become evident as you model each concept and as students plan, organize, and prepare their newspaper for publication.

Although the main thrust of this unit is writing, other communication arts and their complementary roles in the effective use of language cannot be ignored or underplayed. Two of the communication processes that will be utilized extensively in this unit are reading and writing. Pappas, Kiefer, and Levstik (1995) state that

> reading is an active, constructive, social, meaning-making process that consists of a range of transactions with texts during which readers ask questions, monitor understanding or partial understanding of particular texts, and take control of their reading processes. Transactions such as these

foster abilities to question the authority of texts and to read critically and creatively.... The writing process is also an active, constructive, social, meaning-making enterprise. Drawing on their own schemas (which include their knowledge of the language system and the conventions of a range of written genres) writers create texts for readers to use. Because they have to decide what to include in their texts and how to express their messages, the writing process itself engenders in writers new ideas and insights, new meanings, and a deeper thinking. (p. 215)

Graves (1994) states that "Writing is the making of reading. If we know how to construct reading through writing, we will better understand how to take reading apart" (p. 282).

The idea that reading is one subject and writing is another subject seems to disregard our intentions to help students connect the processes, when in fact, students are experiencing this interrelatedness as they write and read. Pappas, Kiefer, and Levstik (1995) discuss how readers and writers are involved with one another by stating,

A writer must always keep the reader in view in composing or constructing text; otherwise, the reader would never be able to interpret the writer's message. And the reader must constantly construct in reading what he or she believes to be the writer's message. Both readers and writers construct written texts; both are involved in problem-solving processes as they create meanings for some purpose. With any use of a written text, there is a reader-writer contract by which particular readers and writers achieve intersubjectivity in written communication. (p. 19)

Calkins (1983) eloquently discusses the connection between reading and writing as she reports her observations of students' writing:

There was no way I could watch writing without reading. While composing, children read continually. They read to savor the sounds of their language, they read to see what they had written, they read to regain momentum, they read to reorient themselves, they read to avoid writing. They read to find gaps in their work, they read to evaluate whether the piece was working, they read to edit. (p. 153)

Calkins goes on to say that as students wrote,

they selected and reselected their main ideas, organized their supporting details, adjusted and defended their sequence. They reached toward inference, they discovered cause and effect, they developed and challenged conclusions. In a sense, everything that happened during writing time related to skills which are traditionally viewed as reading skills. (p. 153)

The process of writing provides an avenue for a deeper understanding of text. Shanahan (1997) states that

reading and writing, as much as any pair of subjects, overlap; that is, they clearly depend on many of the same cognitive elements. You need to know the meanings of many words in order to read *or* write, for example. You need to know something about how sounds and symbols relate. You need to have some ideas about how text relates to the world. (p. 13)

What other communication skills are taught as we study newspapers and informational text? Let's focus on the recursive process of writing and look at how the communication arts are reinforced throughout the unit presented in this book.

The first step in the writing process is *prewriting*—the stage that writers use to generate ideas before they begin to write.

This is the time that the writer defines a purpose for writing (to inform, to persuade, to entertain), selects a topic, organizes and gathers, identifies an audience, and decides on the form of his or her writing (poetry, narrative, report). Pappas, Kiefer, and Levstik (1995) contend, "Prewriting is generating and exploring, recalling and rehearsing, and relating and probing ideas, as well as planning, thinking, and deciding" (p. 215). During the prewriting stage, students should be given opportunities to talk, listen, and ask questions about the topic, or they should read to obtain background information on the topic. During the prewriting stage, students should be encouraged to use mapping, listing, quickwriting, and drawing to plan their writing.

The second stage in the writing process is *drafting*. In this stage, the writer begins to put ideas into words. The writer should concentrate on putting ideas onto paper and should not concentrate on correct spelling, grammar, or punctuation. Reading becomes integral to this process as the writer reads and rereads the initial sketches of the written piece. During the drafting stage, introduce students to computers and word processing programs. Allowing students to use the computer to draft their newspaper articles may be an added incentive for writing. Steelman (1991) examined achievements of middle level students who used computers to write a newspaper. She discovered that the use of the writing process approach is superior to traditional methods of teaching writing and that the use of the computer enhances the process.

The third stage in the writing process is *revision*. During the revision process, the writer reads aloud the draft while others listen to and react to the piece because, as Tompkins (1994) asserts, "Experienced writers...know they must turn to others for reactions and revise on the basis of these comments" (p. 16). Pappas, Kiefer, and Levstik (1995) call revision "re-visioning" and state that during the revision process there are opportunities to "re-think, re-view, re-see, re-make, re-construct, and re-create the text" (p. 216).

Usually, the listener asks questions, provides suggestions, and helps the writer plan revisions. To revise, the writer concentrates on reorganizing paragraphs and sentences, adding or subtracting words, and moving around the words on the page. This is the time that the writer plays with written discourse to refine and polish the message, keeping audience in mind. Dahl and Farnan (1998) claim that "when writers reread their own work with their audience in mind, they reshape ideas in their intended text and discover new ones....The transactive relation between writing and reading leads to critical insights across texts as students generate and express new meanings" (p. 85).

Graves (1994) talks about helping students read their writing: "Deciding what your piece is about is the most basic step in learning to read your own work" (p. 216). He suggests that we help students look for a line that tells what the piece is about. He labels this the "telling line" and indicates that "The 'telling line' is much easier to identify, since it states what the piece is about quite simply and directly" (p. 217). In newspaper writing, this is the lead.

The fourth stage, the *editing* stage, requires refinement of the written work into its published form. Spelling, grammatical, and mechanical errors are addressed and corrected. Proofreading is the major activity during the editing stage. Short, Harste, and Burke (1996) say, "When authors serve as editors of others' writing or have editors talk to them about their own work, they begin to understand the importance of conventions for reading" (p. 126). Again, the communication arts all play important roles in the editing process.

The final step in the writing process is *publishing*. Tompkins (1994) states that "sharing writing is a social activity, and through sharing, children develop sensitivity to the audience and confidence in themselves as writers" (p. 26). Publishing a newspaper is an authentic experience for students in communicating information to a "real" and interested audience. Denman (1995) states

> You cannot get much more authentic than the production of a newspaper.... The newspaper students get the experience of writing not just for a teacher, but for an authentic audience of peers, teachers, administrators, and parents.... The day after an issue comes out, the students return to class eager to share what comments, good or bad, they have heard about the paper. (pp. 55, 57)

Organization of the Book

Each chapter in the book was designed with two sections. The first section familiarizes teachers with the field of journalism and journalistic concepts necessary to teach the individual lessons. The second section contains lessons that are sequenced logically to facilitate students' understanding of journalism, the newspaper, the people who create a newspaper, the news story, the text structures of news stories, and writing news stories for publication. The lessons lead to the creation of a newspaper designed by elementary students that either can be published in their local newspaper, or as a school or class newspaper.

The individual lessons are organized using the following format: Introduction to the Lesson, Modeling by the Teacher, and Practice by the Student. In the Introduction section you will tell the students what they will be learning. In the Modeling section you will demonstrate how to perform this skill or use a particular strategy. You may use the provided figures, examples, and materials in each lesson, or you can design your own materials that are more appropriate for your classroom. In the third section of the lesson, Practice, the students will utilize the new concept on their own or in small groups. Student worksheets for many lessons are provided in Appendix A. Usually the skills or strategies that the students practice will take them on a journey into the world of journalism, in which they will be involved in the writing process—a recursive process of prewriting, drafting, revision, editing, and finally, the ultimate—publishing.

The goal of this book is to heighten students' awareness of the intent and purpose of the newspaper, direct their writing for the newspaper, and aid in the publication of a newspaper. This book is organized into seven chapters. In each chapter, lessons are presented to aid students' understanding of the concepts and vocabulary terms used in the field of journalism.

Chapter One, Background Information for Teachers, provides an overview of the concepts that will be taught in the classroom. Chapter Two, Teaching Journalism Basics, begins with the question, What is a newspaper? This chapter will help students to understand concepts such as newsworthiness, audience, and intent of the newspaper. Identifying audience will help students determine what type of newspaper the class will write—a class newspaper or a school newspaper. A class newspaper should focus on events and students in the class, while a school newspaper should focus on the events and the persons—including students, faculty, and staff—in the school. The audience for a school newspaper might also include the community, if events in the community are tied to events of the school. Students will learn to determine what is considered "news" according to the audience or intent of their newspaper.

Chapter Two also touches on the differences between fact and opinion. Heller (1995) states that "the newspaper is a classic resource for teaching the concepts of fact and opinion, two very important terms to be reckoned with throughout our lifetime" (p. 257). The responsibility of the news reporter is to report the news in an unbiased manner. To achieve this, students need to be able to distinguish between what is factual and what is an opinion.

Chapter Two will introduce students to the people of a newsroom and the roles they play in publishing a newspaper. Shanahan (1997) discusses the idea that readers and writers need to move across disciplines by being exposed to the specialized vocabulary and organizational styles associated with each culture. By studying the terms and the roles of the people of the news, students are brought into the specialized culture of journalism.

Chapter Three, Interviewing, Writing Quotes, and Using Figurative Language, introduces students to techniques that will aid them in collecting information and writing news articles. In the first step—the interview process—student reporters will learn how to interview "real" people, con-

duct the interview, organize the information from the interview, and share that information with the reader. The remaining lessons in the chapter will expose students to using different writing techniques when writing news articles. To report factual information, reporters often quote the opinions and reflections of a particular person. To write in a more interesting and descriptive way, reporters use figurative language such as metaphors and similes. The lessons in the chapter will prepare students to talk and listen to others and to write in an interesting manner.

Chapter Four, Elements and Organizational Structures of News Stories, begins the study of how to structure and write a news story. This chapter includes writing the headline, the lead, and the body of the story. The headline is used to catch the reader's attention. Usually the reader will glance at a headline and then move on to the lead—what Graves (1994) calls the "telling line"—which contains the main ideas of the article. To be able to inform others, the writer needs to capture the readers' interest using a tight lead that contains the article's most important information.

Also included in Chapter Four is an explanation of the organizational structures of news stories, which introduces the study of expository or informational text. Building the story beyond the lead includes organizing the body of the article in a cohesive manner using one of the following organizational structures: Inverted Pyramid, Lead Plus Equal Facts, Chronological Order, Description, and Opinion.

Chapter Five, Writing Different Types of Newspaper Stories, shares the variety of news stories that can be found in a newspaper. Realizing the purpose of each type of story allows students to select a focus for their writing. The different types of news stories take students into the realms of science, sports, entertainment, and cultures by writing columns, editorials, reviews, and reports.

Chapter Six, The Final Steps: Revision, Editing, Layout, and Publication, focuses on the key stages of making a newspaper worthy of reading. Students will want to share their articles with peers and teachers to establish that their articles have achieved their purpose for the intended audience. Revision and editing are important because the writer's pride is at stake. Short, Harste, and Burke (1996) state that "as writers read and reread their pieces to themselves and others, they also begin to self-edit their writing. Self-editing involves attending to conventional aspects such as spelling, grammar, punctuation, and capitalization" (pp. 120–121). The lessons in this chapter make self-editing and peer editing exercises in writing, reading, speaking, and listening.

Gathering information and writing articles for a classroom newspaper would be incomplete if the students were not involved in the layout and design of the paper itself. The remaining lesson in Chapter Six covers aspects of the composing room and the publication of the newspaper. To understand the layout and design process, students should be exposed to the activities associated with the composing room, as well as the roles that key people play in planning the layout, design, and publication of the newspaper. The activity in this part of the chapter provides instruction in vocabulary in a manner in which students become involved in the use and application of these vocabulary terms.

Chapter Seven, Student Evaluation of Unit Concepts, provides a culminating activity for ending the study of newspaper concepts. Because the published newspaper will serve as the summative evaluation for this unit, involving students in an activity that reviews the concepts and key terms will provide a pressure-free way to close the unit. The lesson in this chapter presents a game that reviews the vocabulary and key concepts introduced in the book's preceding lessons.

This book will help you take your students on a journey through the communication arts (speaking, reading, writing, and listening). Through efforts to understand others and their stories, students will talk and learn to listen to others, to collect stories, and to respond to written text. They will be exposed to informational text and how to write to inform an audience. Students will learn how to present information so that others can learn and understand their writing, and students will learn how to present their thoughts in a coherent and organized way. They will read and reread what others have written, and they will expand their vocabulary with the study of terms from another discipline. Hence, the creation of a newspaper in an elementary classroom incorporates study and exploration of communication in an authentic and purposeful way. The unit presented in this book is unique in that students will learn about the newspaper and the field of journalism, while expanding their vocabulary and extending their knowledge of expository text.

Chapter One

Background Information for Teachers

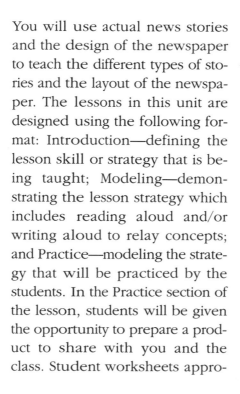

THIS CHAPTER is designed to help you, the teacher, become familiar with the journalistic style of writing, journalism terminology, and the newspaper in general. Before you begin a unit on creating a classroom newspaper, place copies of newspapers in the classroom for the students to read.

You will use actual news stories and the design of the newspaper to teach the different types of stories and the layout of the newspaper. The lessons in this unit are designed using the following format: Introduction—defining the lesson skill or strategy that is being taught; Modeling—demonstrating the lesson strategy which includes reading aloud and/or writing aloud to relay concepts; and Practice—modeling the strategy that will be practiced by the students. In the Practice section of the lesson, students will be given the opportunity to prepare a product to share with you and the class. Student worksheets appropriate for some lessons are provided in Appendix A.

Definition of a Newspaper

A newspaper is a printed document that contains current news, articles, opinions, features, and advertisements. The newspaper can be distributed daily, weekly, or less frequently, and contains three kinds of news: (1) public news, such as meetings, deaths, births, and sports; (2) investigative news, such as behind-the-scenes pieces that uncover information; and (3) analysis, such as columns and editorials that contain opinions based on events.

What Is News?

The following quotes reflect different views of news:

- "anything that will make people talk" (Charles A. Dana, former editor of the *New York Sun*)
- "anything that makes a reader say, 'Gee, whiz!'" (Arthur McEwan, former editor of the *San Francisco Examiner*)
- "anything you can find out today that you didn't know before" (Turner Catledge, former managing editor of *The New York Times*)
- "the first rough draft of history" (Benjamin Bradlee, former executive editor of the *Washington Post*)
- "stories that are original, distinctive, romantic, thrilling, unique, curious, quaint, humorous, odd and apt-to-be-talked-about" (Joseph Pulitzer, former editor of the *St. Louis Post-Dispatch*) (quoted in Hough, 1984).

The *angle* or *news peg* is the reason why the reporter is writing a story; why it is significant, important, or interesting; why it is news. The news peg is the story's main point. Factors or qualities that make a story newsworthy include:

timeliness of the event

season of the event (i.e., holiday, summer)

proximity to the audience

extent of the audience

prominence of the subject in the story

consequences of an event or situation

human interest element (i.e., unusual, provocative, emotional, dramatic, surprising, suspenseful, disastrous, or humorous)

Types of News Articles

News stories include objective stories on topics such as significant events, politics and government, elections, fires, disasters, crime, wars, economics, business, science, religion, health, technology, and local or community events (such as school news, births/deaths, community programs, weddings, grand openings or closings, meetings and speeches, court records). News should be reported without the writer's own feelings or opinions present.

Feature stories are not usually about a subject that is late-breaking news but is of general interest, is odd or unusual, or is entertaining. Often times emotion plays a big part in a feature. A feature is less formal than a straight news story; it's a creative, sometimes subjective article designed primarily to entertain or inform readers of an event, person, situation, or aspect of life. Reviews are feature stories that give a general overview about a television show, movie, play, or musical event.

Photographs can stand alone as newsworthy items, or be used to accompany a corresponding story to help readers visualize the story. Dramatic scenes and emotions such as fear, humor, and sympathy, often times are better expressed in a photograph. The photo itself tells a story. Appealing news pictures can stand alone if the corresponding cutlines (captions) give you the supporting news and details of the picture; the cutline adds depth and meaning to the picture.

Sports stories recap the results of an athletic contest, profile an athlete for his or her accomplishments, or address recreational activities.

The opinion page contains columns, editorials, and letters to the editor, all of which provide a forum for public discourse. Letters to the editor express the subjective thoughts, feelings, and opinions of readers.

Editorials are persuasive pieces that express the opinion of the newspaper or an editor regarding a certain subject. Columns are articles that contain opinions written in first person. Some columnists have become famous because their columns are so well known. For example, Ann Landers and Abigail Van Buren (Dear Abby) write advice columns; Dave Barry writes humorous anecdotes about everyday life; Dick Bragg is a distinguished syndicated feature writer; John Burns is famous for his international reporting; Mitch Album is noted for his sports writing; and Roger Ebert is a syndicated movie reviewer.

Non-story sections of the newspaper include comics and advertisements. Comics are a narrative series of cartoons that provoke humor or amusement. Display advertisements usually are purchased by companies and organizations. They use drawings, photographs, graphic illustrations, and words to publicize new products or services, and to announce special promotions, events, or sales. Display ads appear throughout newspaper pages. The revenue generated from the sales of display ads becomes a source of income for the paper.

Classified ads, however, appear in their own section of a newspaper (usually the back pages or later sections of the paper). The classified section has appropriate headings to classify products and services being listed—Help Wanted, Automotive, Real Estate, Rentals, Rummage Sales, and Jobs. Classified ads are also purchased, with rates based generally on the number of letters or lines used to convey the message. In comparison to display ads, classified ads are less expensive and affordable to the general public.

Parts of a News Story

A headline is the caption above a story that accurately and completely summarizes the contents of the story. Headlines are set off by using larger type; the bigger the type, the more prominent the story.

When writing a headline, consider these guidelines:

Include a verb.

Use active voice, not passive voice.

State or imply a complete sentence in the present tense, but you can leave out articles such as *a* and *the*.

Be accurate.

Capture the full meaning and thrust of the story.

Be concrete and as specific as possible.

Punctuate correctly.

Do not repeat key words.

Do not oversimplify.

Do not emphasize minor points.

Do not overplay or underplay a subject, giving it too much or too little emphasis.

A byline is the name of the writer (and his or her role with the paper), which appears at the head of a news story or with a photograph.

The lead is the most important sentence or paragraph in an article. It is similar to a thesis statement. Do not bury the lead by hiding it in the middle of your story. The lead draws the reader into the story. When writing leads, the reporter includes the Five Ws and the One H.

The first "W" stands for *what*. What happened is usually the most important element of a lead sentence or paragraph. *What* leads seem to be the most frequently used because these leads concentrate on the main event of the story.

The second "W" is *who*. *Who* leads are the easiest to write, but writers should not start a sentence with a name unless the person is easily recognized or is distinctly set off from others. *Who* leads are also commonly used leads because they focus on the most important information being conveyed—the person or people involved in the event.

The third "W" is *when*. When the action took place is almost always in a lead, but stories are not always written chronologically. Instead, most leads start with the most recent condition or development and work backward to develop the story.

The fourth "W" is *where*. *Where* leads are hardly ever used because location is generally not the most significant element of the event. Any local element is often implied or stated in a story. However, if the event is occurring in the future, the lead should be specific about a location.

And finally are the *why* and *how* leads. These leads usually do not contain the most important information. *How* leads are difficult to write because an explanation as to how the event occurred is sometimes not known, too difficult or technical to convey, or too routine to be worth mentioning first. *Why* leads are also difficult to write. If the information for the *why* lead is known, it usually requires presenting several supporting details so the story is not too vague. When explaining a *why*, the reporter must also guard against placing blame on someone. Only if a *why* question can be answered—and it is the major cause of an event or a motive for action—should it be used as the lead.

The body of a news story elaborates on facts given in the lead. The body of the story is organized using different expository text structures: Inverted Pyramid, Lead Plus Equal Facts, Chronological Order, Description, and Opinion. (The lessons in Chapter Four will help teach these text structures more thoroughly.)

Inverted Pyramid is used in general news stories. The story is written with a strong lead, followed by the most important facts and information in the first two paragraphs. The succeeding paragraphs, which might not be read by a hurried reader, continue to develop and support the lead by giving additional details in order of decreasing importance. When the copy editor lays out the story in the designated space, he or she can cut the story from bottom up because all of the most important information should be at the beginning of the story.

Lead Plus Equal Facts is used in interpretative, instructive, or informational news stories. The news is at the top of the story, summarized in the lead, and the continuing story explains the facts in the lead. Quite often the body of the story will consist of background facts contained in previous stories, as well as quoted opinions and supporting information. The facts contained in the body are of equal value and importance, so the entire story should be read.

Chronological Order is used in many types of news stories. A chronological story starts with a lead, followed by paragraphs consisting of events that occurred in a sequence. Human interest stories (those that develop from an extraordinary event, or entertain, or appeal to our emotions) are often times written chronologically. Generally, sports stories present an outcome, significant plays, outstanding players and strategies, followed by a chronological recap of the game by innings, periods, or quarters. Obituaries are often written chronologically. Court and crime stories, and weather, disaster, and accident stories often follow a sequence based on a timeline of when things happened. How-to stories, which provide directions or instructions to a reader, are also written in a step-by-step, chronological manner.

Description is used in features that are written to show how a place affects a person. The reader can visualize similarities in what he is reading compared to what he has experienced; ideas are made concrete. A good descriptive story will use specific nouns, adjectives, and verbs to create vivid pictures, sounds, and feelings for the reader. This type of story includes colors, size dimensions (how long, how big), sounds and noise levels, brightness and darkness, and textures and air quality (temperature, smells). Similes and metaphors can also be used in a descriptive piece. Travel stories, historical pieces, reviews, and personality profiles are examples of stories that use descriptive organization.

Opinion is used in essays or editorials. Facts are supported with facts and reality, but express an opinion with the intent to persuade or influence the reader or to promote change. The general format is to state a problem, examine its components (present the facts, compare, and contrast), then offer a solution. A well-written opinion piece presents clear, logical thinking, using accurate information, to make its point without preaching.

Quotes are what a person said, directly or indirectly. A direct quote is the speaker's exact words, verbatim, enclosed in quotation marks. Indirect quotes are words that paraphrase something that a person said.

An ending or conclusion is not always necessary for a news story. However, if one is written, it usually tells the story's main point, reiterates the significance of the information presented in the lead and body, or ties up loose ends. Feature stories and those written chronologically usually have a conclusion.

People in the Newsroom

The *publisher* owns or controls the newspaper.

The *editor in chief* is in charge of deciding what news goes into the paper. This person supervises the news, sports, and features, their reporters, and the copy editors.

The *managing editor* is usually the second in command, behind the editor in chief. The managing editor assists the editor in chief in determining what news goes into the paper—local, state, national, international—and helps pick comics, photos, syndicated material, and features to include.

The *advertising manager* oversees the representatives who sell advertising to businesses.

The *news editor* is in charge of determining what stories are newsworthy and assigns reporters to write stories.

The *reporter* is the person who is assigned to write a story; he or she gathers information by attending an event, doing research, and interviewing those involved. This person writes a story that tells what happened, answering the Five Ws and

One H. A reporter should be skilled at observing, listening, taking notes, asking questions, doing research, fact-checking, and interpreting information.

A *columnist* writes articles that contain opinions or first-person accounts.

The *copy editor* checks the entire story for accuracy, to see that there are no factual, spelling, or grammatical errors. This person also rewrites and revises, corrects any errors in the story, and writes a headline. This person should be detail-oriented, have strong knowledge of the language, and have a broad-based general knowledge.

The *proofreader* reads the proof pages and marks errors for correction.

The *photographer* takes pictures to illustrate a story. Sometimes the picture stands alone without a story. This is called a feature or news photo, depending on its content.

Summary

This chapter is intended for teachers and is an overview of journalism concepts that will be taught in the lessons that follow. Understanding what is newsworthy, the types of news articles in a newspaper, parts of the news story, and the people of the newsroom provides the foundation for the creation of a classroom newspaper. The next chapter will help you to assess your students' knowledge of these concepts as you begin teaching journalism basics.

Chapter Two

Teaching Journalism Basics

INCLUDED IN this chapter is a discussion of the type of newspaper that the students will create in the unit, as well as the newspaper's audience and intent. Typically, students will think of topics they are familiar with, but sometimes students do not have the resources and the background knowledge to write on these topics. When talking about students' writing from experiential

knowledge, Graves (1994) states, "I try to connect what Jason knows, as shown in his writing, with where his knowledge comes from. I try to elicit the history behind his knowing. Children need to know the roots of their knowledge" (p. 85). A discussion of who will be reading the newspaper and what this audience will be interested in reading about might help direct students to select topics that are within their experiences so that students can readily obtain information.

The students in both of the fourth-grade classrooms described in this book decided that they would write a school newspaper. A brainstorming session of topics included topics that were outside

their experiential realm, but discussion of how to obtain information for the news stories and the target audience helped students narrow their topics to school events, school people, and elementary-age related topics.

The activities in this chapter will introduce students to the newspaper, will help students understand what is news and not news, will help students identify facts or opinions, and will introduce the roles of the people who work for the newspaper. At the end of this chapter, students will be invited to apply for the various positions for the school newspaper (see Student Worksheet 1 on page 63).

Assessment of Existing Knowledge

To begin the unit, you should assess the students' existing knowledge of the newspaper using a brainstorming session. Ask students, "What is a newspaper?" Record responses to this session on chart paper or on the board. After this session, give students copies of a complete newspaper to examine. After they are given a chance to browse and explore the newspaper, ask them to revise their brainstormed list, changing and updating their chart with any new information.

Introduce the unit to students by sharing with them that they will be writing articles for a newspaper. Share with students that they will each take part in designing the newspaper. They will be involved in the field of journalism—the profession of reporting and publishing news for the public to read. Share titles of newspapers and discuss the titles. Also, explain that the newspaper's name and date of publication, as well as the volume and issue numbers, appear on the first page in the title plate, which is also called the newspaper's *flag* or *banner*. For example, the flags of these U.S. newspapers could be shared: *The New York Times, Washington Post, USA Today, Star Tribune, Dallas Morning News, San Diego Daily Transcript, San Francisco Chronicle, Colorado Springs Gazette, Raleigh News and Observer, Chicago Tribune,* and *San Francisco Examiner.* Examples of international English-language newspapers include *Sidney Morning Herald, Yorkshire Evening Post,* and the *Toronto Star.*

Discuss the terms *gazette, chronicle, observer, transcript, inquirer, journal,* and *examiner* as related to news and reporting.

Define a few of the terms and ask students to explain why these terms have been used for the titles of newspapers. For example, explain that *gazette* is a British term used to describe a publication that contains announcements and bulletins; the term *chronicle* means to recount or record information; to *observe* means to notice, comment, or remark about a happening; and a *transcript* is an official written account of something. Share the flags of a few newspapers, and ask students to brainstorm why they think these terms were used in the titles. The class may wish to come up with a title for its newspaper and create a flag. In two fourth-grade classrooms that used this unit, the students voted on the title of their newspaper.

What Is the News?

Share with students the definition of *news.* News is a report of new information, especially about recent happenings or recognizable people. There are many reasons why something is newsworthy: it is current, happening now; it has seasonal appeal; the audience is interested in it and it is important to the readers; or it is unusual, surprising, or humorous. During this discussion, introduce students to where we can find news—television, magazines, newspaper, radio. Discuss the differences in the format of these types of news sources. Discuss the differences between international, national, state, city, school, and class news.

Share with students that while the newspaper contains factual information as found in news stories, public notices, and classified ads, it also contains opinions such as in articles found on the editorial page and in advice columns. Helping students determine the differences between fact and opinion is key to helping them understand what is reported in these sections. Students should be aware that facts are accounts of what really happened. Facts can be documented and verified. Opinions, on the other hand, are what one thinks about a subject. These thoughts are not based on what really happened, but on what the writer interprets or believes. Lesson 2 on page 18 will help students learn the difference between fact and opinion.

People in the Newsroom

A word game could be used to introduce students to the people who work on the newspaper, including publisher, editor in chief, managing editor, photographer, proofreader, reporter, news editor, copy editor. (See Lesson 3 on page 19.) Ask students to volunteer for the roles of photographer, reporters, editors, copy editors, and the composing room staff. Share with students journalistic terminology that is associated with each role. For example, terms that are used by the reporter include: *scoop, resources, end mark, one last check, objective, hard news, fact error, cover, beat, attribution, assignment,* and *dictionary.* Terms used in the composing room are *deadline* and *dummy;* terms used by the copy editor are *cut* and *typo.*

Summary

The concepts discussed in this chapter have direct applications to other content areas. For example, in science students need to be able to determine what information is based on fact and what is based on opinion. Science, as a discipline, is based on facts, which can be verified. In social studies, however, what others think—opinions—can be helpful in understanding an event, but what is known to be true—facts—contributes to the significance of the event. Understanding the roles that people play in creating a newspaper and the roles in other professions will make students realize that the society we live in is very extensive and all-encompassing.

LESSON #1

News Versus Not News

Heather Hagner and Jessica Bresnahan

Introduction Ask the students, "What is news?" List their ideas on the board. Through the discussion, students will learn that a news story tells readers about an important or unusual event.

Modeling Brainstorm a list of potential news story ideas before the lesson. In front of the class, separate each story idea into one of two columns, under the headings News and Not News. Tell students why each story is or is not news.

News	Not News
"Price of School Lunch Increases"	"Tommy Scraped His Knee on the Playground"
"The Chicken Eggs in the Science Room Hatched Today"	"A Pencil Was Found in the Hallway Today"
"The Major Will Be Speaking at the Assembly on Friday"	"Mr. Jones Is Wearing Blue Socks Today"

Practice The students will break into groups of three or four. Each group will create five story ideas that would be considered news stories and five that would not. (Because students have identified the type of newspaper that they will be creating, the ideas listed might include topics that would be applicable for their newspaper.) Ask each group to exchange lists with another group, then determine which story ideas fit into the category of News and which are Not News. One student will record the ideas in two columns, under the headings News and Not News. (See Student Worksheet 1 on page 63.)

LESSON 2

Fact Versus Opinion

Angie Halverson and Aimee Sprecher

Introduction

It is important for students to recognize the difference between fact and opinion statements. Opinion statements are beliefs, views, and judgments. Explain that facts are pieces of information that can be proven by actual evidence. Some possible words that show opinion are *should, could, think, feel, best, worst,* or anything that is considered subjective. This lesson will encourage critical thinking skills by asking the following:

Why is it important to know the difference between fact and opinion as a consumer, citizen, and student?

When do we rely on the facts and opinions of others in daily life?

When do we use fact and opinion?

Have opinion articles (for example, letter to the editor, editorial column, reviews) and factual articles (for example, news stories, sports stories) available to show as examples.

Modeling

Read aloud a statement and ask students whether it is fact or opinion. Some examples are as follows:

It is 32 degrees outside today. (fact)

It is too cold outside. (opinion)

I can't teach because it is too bright. (opinion)

Apples are nutritious. (fact)

Apples taste good. (opinion)

Snoopy is a witty dog. (opinion)

Practice

Group students in pairs, then pass out various articles. They will read the articles and decide if the articles contain statements that are fact or opinion. Students will keep a list of statements that indicate whether the article is fact or opinion.

Ask students to share their lists of statements from articles in a large-group discussion. Write each statement in the proper category on the chalkboard.

LESSON 3
People of the Newsroom
Emily Tackes, Jenny Marx, and Sara Scherer

Introduction

This lesson will help the students become familiar with the people in the newsroom and their specific roles.

Using semantic mapping, have the students brainstorm the roles of each person involved. This includes Publisher, Editor, News Editor, Reporter, Columnist, Copy Editor, Proofreader, and Photographer. An example of a semantic web can be seen in Figure 1; see also Student Worksheet 2 on page 64.

Figure 1—Semantic Web of Reporter's Roles

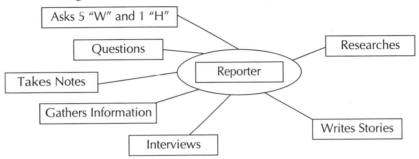

After each role is brainstormed, as a class come up with a working definition for each role.

Modeling

Divide the class into seven groups. Give each group a role and the definition of that role. The groups should be Editor, News Editor, Reporter, Columnist, Copy Editor, Proofreader, Photographer. You will role play what the publisher does and the class will guess which role you are playing. Each group will then come up with a role play for its role and show the class. They can use gestures, voices, and props to role play. The rest of the class will guess which person the group is acting out.

Practice

Before the activity, prepare pieces of paper with the different roles labeled on them. To begin the activity, tape a piece of paper on the back of each child. (You may have to duplicate roles depending on the number of students.) The children will then ask their classmates "yes" or "no" questions to determine what role they are. They are to record their findings on a piece of paper with columns labeled "I Am" and "I Am Not" until they determine their role.

After students have gained an understanding of the roles, hand out job applications for each student to "apply" for one of the positions studied (see Student Worksheet 3–Application for a Newspaper Position on page 65). Students will have to choose a position and explain their qualifications for the intended job.

LESSON 4

The Reporter

Shirin Kukanich and Margaret Sauer

Introduction

Tell students that the class will be learning vocabulary used by newspaper reporters. Many of the students will be reporters during this newspaper unit, so they should be familiar with these terms. As students begin to understand the role of the reporter, they could brainstorm questions to ask a reporter. (*The New York Times* Web site has an interactive page called "Ask a Reporter," http://www.nytimes.com/learning/students/.)

Modeling

Read some of the new vocabulary from the list that follows.

New vocabulary words used by a reporter:

angle	end mark
assignment	fact error
attribution	hard news
beat	objective
cover	one last check
deadline	scoop
dictionary	

Choose one of the words and write a sentence on the board using that word.

"The reporter *beat* the eggs for breakfast."

The students are to decide if the word *beat* in the example sentence is used as part of a reporter's vocabulary.

The class can look in their Glossary of Newspaper Terms (see Appendix E) to decide if the word is following the journalism definition.

Ask students to think of a new sentence that uses *beat* as part of a reporter's vocabulary. For example, "The reporter's beat was the high school."

Practice

Have students complete Student Worksheet 4–Reporter Vocabulary Quiz on page 66. The students will read the sentences with the italicized word and decide if the word is used as part of a reporter's vocabulary by comparing it to the glossary definition. If the word is used correctly, the students will leave it. If it does not use the correct definition, they will write a new sentence that uses the word correctly.

20

Chapter Three

Interviewing, Writing Quotes, and Using Figurative Language

The Interview

THE FIRST section of this chapter will teach students how to interview others. The interview process is socially oriented and involves interaction with others and interpersonal relationships. Students will learn how to relate to others, how to obtain information and report it in an unbiased way, and how to respect the feelings and rights of others. The skills introduced here can be transported to any area of life as young students interact and respond to others.

Have students brainstorm ways they can obtain information from others outside the school. Field trips, guest speakers, or e-mail are all methods that could be introduced as ways to find out about others.

Using Quotes and Figurative Language

In this section, students will learn how to write in an interesting way, so that others will want to read what they have written. Quotes and figurative language are literary elements that are used in all areas of written discourse—both informative text and narrative text. If students master the use of quotes and descriptive language, they can use these literary elements as they read, speak, or write in any genre.

A quote is what a person said, directly or indirectly. Direct quotes are words enclosed in quotation marks that indicate the exact words that were said by the person; indirect quotes paraphrase something that the person said.

Similes are figures of speech that make comparisons using the words *like* or *as*. Metaphors are figures of speech that compare two different things without using a word of comparison, such as *like* or *as*. Similes and metaphors bring writing to life. These figures of speech are used most often in sports and feature articles.

Summary

Once students complete the lessons in this chapter, they will know how to collect information in order to write a thorough, interesting news story. They will also know how to write well using figurative language, which is a skill that will carry over into all areas of writing and learning.

LESSON 5
Conducting an Interview
Betsy Roehl and Lynn Helgeson

Introduction

Begin this lesson by introducing the interview process to students. Explain that the interview process is important for the reporter. The reporter must obtain accurate information and use this information in the article that he or she is writing. The interview process includes planning the interview, conducting the interview, sharing results, and writing the article. Students should understand the importance of an interview prior to writing a news story.

Modeling

Discuss and demonstrate the steps in the interview process:

1. Plan the interview:
   - Arrange a time, date, and place for the interview. (You can arrange a mock interview with a person the class is currently studying.)
   - Plan questions to ask. (Students can brainstorm possible questions to ask. In your directions, stress that students should ask questions about things they do not know and need to find out about.)
   - Select questions to ask. (Explain the importance of avoiding questions that can be answered with just "yes" or "no.")
   - Write questions on notecards. (Write the remaining questions on notecards to be used in the mock interview.)
   - Sequence cards in the order of how questions should be asked.

2. Conduct the interview:
   - Greet the person. (Conduct a mock interview with a student who will assume the role of the person students are currently studying.)
   - Ask prewritten questions from notecards.
   - Always take notes on responses to questions. (Stress the importance of collecting direct quotes.)
   - Ask follow-up questions for answers that are not clear, but be sure that you protect the feelings of the interviewee.
   - End the interview and thank the interviewee.

3. Share results:
   - Write a newspaper article. (Share an example of a news article that was written from an interview, emphasizing direct quotes and other important parts of a news story from the interview.)

(continued)

L E S S O N 5 *(continued)*

Practice

Provide the steps of the interview process for students to refer to on an overhead, chalkboard, or handout.

Ask students to role-play the interview process in pairs in which one student is the interviewer, and one student is the person interviewed. Students may assume the role of a person from history or a person in the news today, or they may be themselves. Emphasize that students should follow the steps of the interview process while they conduct their interview. Students will then create a newspaper article from their interview.

LESSON 6
Writing Quotes
Jennifer Belcher, Polly LaMontagne, and Lisa Schiltz

Introduction

Write a set of quotation marks on the board and ask the class if anyone knows what these marks mean. When someone identifies them as quotation marks, tell the class that quotations are used in writing to show what someone said.

Modeling

Display an overhead with a paragraph from a newspaper article that contains at least one direct quotation. Then ask the students to find the quote in the article, and you can highlight the quote in the passage.

At this time, identify this quotation as a direct quote, and inform the class that a direct quote contains a speaker's exact words. You may also tell the class that sometimes a speaker's words are paraphrased; this is an indirect quote.

Now demonstrate how to write a direct quote by asking a student an open-ended question like, "Tell me about the football game last night." Record the student's response and write it as a direct quote on the overhead.

> "The team lost the game," remarked Joe.
>
> or
>
> Joe said, "The team lost the game."

Identify the phrases "remarked Joe" and "Joe said" as speech tags. Explain that a comma must be used before or after a speech tag, depending on its location in the sentence. Also, it is important that punctuation used in the quote is enclosed in the quotation marks.

Practice

Group students into pairs, and give each pair an open-ended question to ask each other. Each member of the pair will interview the other by asking the question and recording the response as a direct quote on a blank overhead transparency. Once all pairs are ready, have them share their responses with the class. (For examples of quotes included in an article, see the human interest story "County humane society offers winter pet care tips" on page 45.)

LESSON 7
Writing Metaphors and Similes
Sarah Sykes and Lynn Ludwig

Introduction Similes are figures of speech that make comparisons using the words *like* or *as* (e.g., "His home run ball flew out of the park like a bird."). Metaphors are figures of speech comparing two different things without using a word of comparison (e.g., Peace is a sunrise). Descriptive words enliven writing. This lesson helps students understand and practice using similes and metaphors.

Modeling First, state metaphor examples such as

Thunder is someone bowling.
Thunder is a giant laughing.
Thunder is elephants playing.

Now state examples of similes, such as

Quick as a fox.
Quick as a streak of lightning.
Quick as an instant breakfast.

Explain the difference between these two figures of speech to the class.

Practice Ask students to contribute their ideas to complete the incomplete statements that follow:

"A newspaper is..."

and

"Morning is..."

Then ask students to contribute their ideas to complete the following similes:

"A homework assignment is like..."

and

"Slow as..."

Chapter Four

Elements and Organizational Structures of News Stories

THIS SECTION of the unit takes students right into writing news articles. In this chapter students will learn how to grab the reader's attention with tight headlines and solid leads, and they will learn how to write the body of the story. Understanding this information will help students learn and study how writers organize and present information in expository text, which is characteristic of how many content area texts are written.

This chapter also introduces students to informational text and its purpose. Students will learn how the reporter shares facts on a topic. Students also will be exposed to various text structures that best relay information to an audience. This introduction to expository text can be used not only in the newspaper unit, but can serve as an introduction to the text structures used in content areas such as social studies, science, and math.

Elements of a News Story

The news story is organized with different parts, including the headline, the byline, the lead, and the body. The newspaper story that will be tracked in this section was written by a group of fourth graders. This class first brainstormed ideas for their newspaper and then volunteered to write the various articles. For this article on pet care in the winter, the students decided to bring in a guest speaker, the director of the local humane society, and they wrote the article based on what the guest speaker shared with the class.

The byline indicates who wrote the story; it's the name of the writer or writers (and their roles with the paper) appearing at the beginning of a news story or along with a photograph. These students included photographs with the story; the pictures captured the guest speaker and scenes from the classroom.

The Headline

The headline is the first thing the reader sees, so it has to grab attention. A headline is a summarizing phrase that captures the essence of the news story. Before students begin to write their own headlines, have them look at news stories from their local newspaper that do not have headlines. Instruct students to brainstorm headlines for these news stories, then share their headlines with their peers. Ask them which headlines grabbed their attention and which did not.

The Lead

The lead is the most important aspect of an article. It lays the foundation for the article and usually answers who, what, where, when, why, and how. It appears in the first paragraph of a story and (1) tells the reader what the story is about, (2) makes the reader want to read on by capturing his or her attention, and (3) creates a mood.

The lead holds all the essential facts—the Five Ws and the One H—putting the most important one first. (Who was involved? What happened? Where did it occur? When did it occur? Why did it happen? How did it happen?) A lead should be short, brief, and clear, but not loaded down with too many facts. A lead sentence should never have more than 25 words, and no lead paragraph should have more than 35 words. Good leads contain strong, active verbs. Share with students some different types of leads, such as

narrative (anecdote) lead: a good type of lead for a feature story

shocking statement lead: surprises or teases the reader

description lead: sets the scene for the story

informative lead: gets right to the point; generally used for a news story

direct address lead: involves the reader by using the word *you*

question lead: asks a question, but is difficult to write and is often a cliché

surprise/enigma lead: teases the reader, but the headline sometimes gives away the surprise

quotation lead: begins with a direct or indirect quote that gives one of the important facts in the words of a key witness or subject

Quote leads are not the best to use because they often do not provide a quick, clear, summary of the story. However, if the source has provided a succinct, compelling, insightful quote that captures and summarizes the situation, the quote can be used. What is said has to be more important than who said it.

Share examples of leads that fit into each category. Have students collect leads of the stories for which they collected headlines. Following are the leads that correspond with the headlines that will be used in Lesson 8 on page 30:

Headline: Lake Michigan yields a Texas-sized coho

Lead: The state's largest coho salmon came this close (hold your index fingers ¼ inch apart) from being steamed in white wine with a little dill sauce on the side. (surprise lead)

Headline: City's oldest house to get makeover

Lead: Congratulations on your new home, Patrick Moore. (direct address lead)

Headline: Light showers bring a gloomy end to summer vacation

Lead: Cloudy and sometimes wet weather was expected to stick around southeastern Wisconsin today, hardly Eden-like conditions, for the Lilith Fair or a nice final day of summer vacation for students of Milwaukee Public Schools and some suburban schools. (description lead)

Headline: Desert survival

Lead: Sydney, Australia—In an extraordinary end to a bizarre search, an American tourist has been found alive after being lost for 40 days in West Australia's Great Sandy desert, one of the most hostile landscapes in the world whose average day-time temperature is 90 degrees Fahrenheit. (informative lead)

As writers, we all use leads for our pieces. For example, in writing about a science experiment, students can use their major conclusion as a summary lead. In social studies, after studying a particular historical event, students could write a lead statement, followed by a chronological listing of events. Therefore, the lessons in this chapter should help students to understand that no matter what we write, we need to "catch" our reader's attention.

The body of the news story contains all of the facts or opinions and the ending. The Five Ws and the One H are covered more thoroughly, and details are explained in the body of the story.

Organizational Structures of News Stories

Students will learn how to organize their thoughts by stating the essence of their story in the lead, then organizing the

details to relay information. The organizational style of the text also reflects the intent of the article and relays the story's information in an organized and understandable fashion. Some articles are best organized using a chronological presentation of facts, while others are organized by describing details or elements of the topic.

There are five ways to organize a news story: Inverted Pyramid, Lead Plus Equal Facts, Chronological Order, Description, Opinion. Sometimes these organizational structures can be applied to assist the comprehension of content materials. The lessons that follow will introduce students to these five organizational structures.

Now that students have all the components of the news story, invite them to draft their story or column. If theclassroom or school has computers and access to word processing programs, add another dimension to this unit by inviting students to prepare their drafts on the computer. Once their drafts are completed, students will be excited to share their writing with others because revising may mean another visit to the computer. Once the draft is completed and the students are comfortable with the message of their news story, they can begin the process of revision with peers and the teacher.

Summary

Knowledge of the various text structures sets the stage for understanding the different types of news stories, and also for understanding the expository text structures used in science, social studies, math, and other types of informational text. The text structure used to organize the news story should coordinate the reporter's message and intent in a logical way.

LESSON 8
Writing Headlines
Angie Anderson and Dan Nortman

Introduction

Students will brainstorm ideas of what a headline contains while you write their ideas on the board and come to a conclusion that a headline is the caption of a story, which accurately summarizes the story's contents. The print of a headline is normally larger than the story's print. The headline is an essential tool in grasping the reader's attention to that article. Therefore, it needs to be as creative and intriguing as possible. Some stories may not seem exciting or adventurous; however, a good headline will hook the reader's interest.

Modeling

Read an article and give it a headline, then write the headline on the board, highlighting its various elements.

> Mrs. Bee returns from London

Make sure students notice the large print and the wording that emphasizes the major points of the article and includes an active verb. These elements draw the reader's attention. Discuss with students why they would want to read an article with this title.

Have students collect headlines from the local newspaper that capture their attention. A discussion of why each headline caught their attention may point out that as individuals, we have differing interests. For example, these headlines that were collected from the *Milwaukee Journal Sentinel* for August 24, 1999, can be shared:

> Lake Michigan yields a Texas-sized coho
> City's oldest house to get makeover
> Light showers bring a gloomy end to summer vacation
> Desert survival

Practice

In pairs, the students will receive a local newspaper article minus the headline. Together they will read the article and come up with three possible headlines. Ask them to share their ideas with the class, and as a group the class will choose its favorite headline for the articles.

Later, ask students to choose an event that occurred that day and to jot down the key ideas to create a headline. If students have trouble coming up with ideas, here are some possible topics:

What I ate for lunch.

What happened this weekend.

Where we took a field trip.

What I did this summer.

When finished, ask students to share their story and headline with the class.

LESSON 9
The Story: Headline, Lead, Body, End
Michelle Schubert, Susan Roe, and Rick Steele

Introduction

Students will be putting together the elements of newspaper stories. Your teaching will focus on the elements of a story, which include the headline, lead, body, and end.

Modeling

Using the article "All the dogs have their day: As moves go, this wasn't bad" (from the *Milwaukee Journal Sentinal*, Tuesday, November 30, 1999; see Appendix B for full article), describe each element of the story. The headline is the caption above the story that summarizes the content of the article and appears in bigger type:

> All dogs have their day: As moves go, this wasn't bad

The lead is the most important sentence in the first paragraph which draws the reader's attention.

> Now it's a humane society.

The body elaborates on facts given in the lead. For example, this article gives the new address, explains the move, and introduces the building's new inhabitants. The body of this article begins in the first paragraph and continues for several paragraphs.

The end retells the story and ties up loose ends. The last two paragraphs in the "All the dogs have their day" article illustrate this very well.

> Here, each dog has a separate room—large enough to entertain prospective adoptive owners. Sunlight from big windows in a common area streams through window and door glass into each room, where each dog can curl up on his own fluffy bed.

> The dogs wouldn't want to live there, but it's a really nice place to visit.

Remind students that stories written for the newspaper are arranged in columns or lines going down the page. The draft of the story does not need to be arranged in this format, but the final draft will need to be arranged in columns.

Practice

Give students one element for a story and ask them to create the other three elements. Different groups will receive a different element to work from. They will then share the complete story that they have designed. The news article that follows was written for *The Wildcat Gazette*.

(continued)

31

Building additions proposed, need vote approval
by Jordan, Andrew, and Cody

We might be adding on to the school in the near future, because the kindergarten classrooms are too small....

"With all-day kindergarten we need more classrooms. We just ran out of space," says Karen Martzahl, a Plover-Whiting kindergarten teacher.

There is currently one kindergarten classroom on the second floor, and Martzahl's is on the first floor. Expansion plans call for three smaller rooms to be added to the building, all on the first floor along the north side, near Mrs. Stenstrom's first-grade classroom.

Because there are also plans to widen Hoover Avenue on the building's west side, the school's main entrance will be moved to the north side of the building, she said. If you see the flagpole, that is where the new main doors will be located. Visitor parking will also be in this area.

The main office will be relocated into the area where the current band room is, off the main doors. The bigger band room will be a new room that is part of the addition.

Residents from Stevens Point and Plover will vote on a referendum for the changes, possibly during April.

"If the voters say 'no, you can't do it,' then we have to come up with another plan," said Martzahl.

The costs for the proposed changes are still being determined, said Principal Bill King.

LESSON 10
Writing a Story Using the Inverted Pyramid Structure
Mark Larson

Introduction

Share with students that today they will learn how to write a news story using the organizational structure called the inverted pyramid. Ask the class to decide on a topic, then collectively list 10 sentence ideas. Each student will use those 10 sentences, using an inverted pyramid format, to organize the body of a story.

Modeling

Have available samples of several newspaper stories that use the inverted pyramid structure. A sample story has been provided here for modeling this type of structure.

Example Story

A fire in the school kitchen set off the sprinkler system at McMahon Elementary School Monday, giving students, staff, and teachers an unexpected half-day off.

No one was injured during the blaze, which caused an estimated $5,000 in damage, according to Jason Hanson, a Stevensville fire fighter. Students were dismissed from school at 11 a.m. due to the smoke and water in the cafeteria, said Walter Hall, principal.

The fire started at 10:30 a.m. when a microwave oven short-circuited, sending sparks that lit a roll of paper towels, Hanson said.

The cooks in the kitchen used a fire extinguisher to fight the fire, but were unable to contain it, said Mary Edwards, McMahon's head cook.

Flames from the fire triggered the school's fire alarm and set off the sprinklers, she said. Students then evacuated the building and, after Hall and the fire department assessed the situation, Hall dismissed the students for the rest of the day.

Classes were expected to be held today, Hall said, adding that the cooks will still be able to use the kitchen while minor repairs are made.

The cooks were making pizza for the students' lunch when the fire started, Edwards said. Wednesday's lunch will be either scorched pizza or torched chicken and burnt mash potatoes, she joked.

This is a great time to point out that most newspaper stories are edited. It is normal, even probable that a story is too long for the column in which it will appear. Stories are chopped or reduced in length from the last paragraph back. Young journalists should not feel insulted if this happens to them. Because many articles are written in an inverted pyramid style, the important facts are at the beginning, so the article will still be useful even if there is not a second page.

Write a news story that uses the inverted pyramid style for its body. Note that the story has a lead that summarizes the story, followed by the rest of the story, in which supporting facts are arranged in descending order. The least impor-

(continued)

33

LESSON 10 *(continued)*

tant or least interesting facts are at the bottom of the story. To illustrate the format, draw an inverted pyramid (standing on its point) to show how the story tapers to a point. Share the example in Figure 2 with students.

Figure 2—Inverted Pyramid Structure

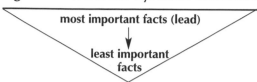

most important facts (lead)

least important facts

Practice

Read a lead from a newspaper story, then give students five factual ideas from the story. Ask students to rearrange the ideas as a class to write a story using an inverted pyramid format. Finally, read the entire original story, so students can see how close they came to the original.

Have students come up with another newsworthy topic to write about, then collectively list 10 facts that can be made into sentences about their topic. Each student will then arrange and write the sentences as a story, using the inverted pyramid form, putting the sentences into descending order of importance. Each student should be prepared to share and explain why he or she wrote the story as he or she did.

In our fourth-grade classroom, students first interviewed a teacher who collects ties, then listed the items that they felt should be included in their article. They organized the items in descending order of importance. Following is the article they wrote.

Collecting Ties With Mr. Hautala
by Wes and Katie

Most boys have 2 or 3 ties, but Mr. Hautala has 6,000 ties in his basement. He gets most of his ties from Goodwill and many other thrift stores. He even takes some plain ones and paints on them.

Also, Mr. Hautala has traded his ties with famous people. He once traded with the TV star who played the judge on *Night Court*.

He got his first tie 10 years ago, but the one that is worth the most to him is a green tie that has a guitar turning into a lady.

He likes to collect ties because it's fun, and people laugh when he wears some of them. He told us he wants to collect as many as he can before he dies.

Maybe, someday you could start collecting ties, and try to collect more than Mr. Hautala. You better start now if you're going to break his record.

LESSON 11
Writing a Story Using a Lead Plus Equal Facts Structure
Jenny Chandler and Nikki Strege

Introduction This lesson will teach students how to write a news story using the pattern Lead Plus Equal Facts. Figure 3 shows how the lead is supported by facts of equal importance in this type of story.

Figure 3—Lead Plus Equal Facts Structure

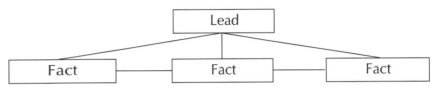

Modeling Place a transparency of Figure 3 on the overhead. With the lead and facts given in the example that follows, explain these concepts as you write a short newspaper article for the class.

Examples of Lead and Fact Sentences

Lead: The cafeteria helpers made a lunch of ham and cheese sandwiches yesterday.
Fact: The cafeteria had smells of ham and cheese flowing through the air.
Fact: The cafeteria just received a shipment of Wisconsin's best cheese.
Fact: The cafeteria was full of happy children with full tummies.
Lead: The baseball player hit his 70th home run for the league's record.
Fact: This record was set in St. Louis, Missouri, with the baseball player's son by his side.
Fact: The home run record was set in 1998.
Fact: The baseball player hit his home run with the fans' support.

Practice Hand out to each student a piece of paper that has either a lead sentence or an equal fact written on it. Direct students to search among one another for the corresponding lead or facts to complete their story. Once the students are in their correct groups of four, define and explain the concept of lead plus equal facts. Explain that the lead sentence must answer the Five Ws and the One H, and the equal facts must support the lead sentence with information to help further explain the story.

Ask students to figure out whether their sentence is a lead or equal fact. These sentences will assist the students in creating their own newspaper articles. The students will then create their own lead sentence and equal facts. Have students present their articles to the class. (See Student Worksheet 5—Writing Lead Plus Equal Facts Articles on page 67.)

LESSON 12
Writing a Story in Chronological Order
Melissa Baran, Mary Bieneck, and Sherri Ronge

Introduction

Share with students that there is order in our world. Order is often conveyed as steps or sequencing. For example, we learn to crawl, walk, and then run; we go to preschool, kindergarten, elementary school, middle school, and then high school. Share an example or two and ask students to think of some others.

Finally, share that stories are often written the same way—in a sequence or order from first to last. A story in chronological order is organized with the lead first, then the sequence of events and additional facts in the body. Meetings and speeches are not covered chronologically, but a sports game recap or a listing of events from a major happening could be written using chronological order.

Modeling

Choose a few current events articles that are written in chronological order to read to the students. Make sure that some of the articles have great leads, while some begin with humorous, shocking, and boring leads. This contrast makes it clear to students what to write and what not to write. Share with students the graphic organizer in Figure 4.

Figure 4—Chronological Order

Read to the class the paragraphs you have chosen. Discuss the students' reactions. Why do they want to continue reading one and not the other? Why are leads important? How are the events in the articles sequenced in chronological order?

Pass out copies of the article titled "All the dogs have their day" (see Appendix B on page 73). Point out the lead. Point out the Five Ws and One H. Point out the first, second, and third events. Point out the conclusion.

Practice

Pass out newspapers to pairs of students, and ask each pair to find their own examples of newspaper articles. Ask students to circle the lead, box the Five Ws and the One H, number the events, and underline the conclusion. Next, ask students to write a story presenting the events of a happening in chronological order.

In an article titled "Wisconsin's Winter Wonderland," Aaron wrote about events in his life in Wisconsin. He organized his article using a collection of things he did in the winter in Wisconsin.

(continued)

Wisconsin's winter wonderland
by Aaron

One day I went snowboarding and my friends taught me lots and lots of tricks.
One day I went skating and I fell and broke my leg.
Another day I went snowmobiling with my dad. I tied a sled to the back of the snowmobile and I rode on the back.
One day I went ice fishing with my mom, and my mom slipped into the water.
One day I went skiing with my best friend, and she fell in the water. We both started to laugh.

LESSON 13
Writing a Descriptive Story
Teri Foerstera and Amy Vander Sanden

Introduction Newspaper articles are organized in many different ways. They may be informational, narrative, explanatory, persuasive, or descriptive. A descriptive story includes both facts and the writer's reactions.

Modeling Read aloud the article with the headline "Dorm room decorating all about making the most of limited space." (See Appendix C on page 75 for article.) Create a semantic map like the one in Figure 5 on the overhead projector using details from the article.

Figure 5—Semantic Map of Dorm Room

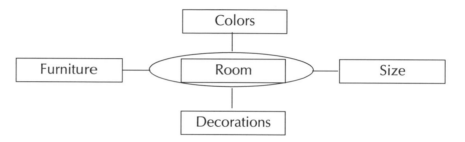

Ask students to select specific details from the article that fit under each category. Record these details on the semantic map on the overhead projector. If more modeling is needed, help students to create a semantic map for the classroom, then ask them to create a descriptive paragraph about the classroom.

Practice Have each student create a semantic map, using the worksheet provided, for his or her bedroom at home. Students can use the detail headings from the model above or create their own headings. Instruct students to write a short descriptive paper about their rooms. Explain to students that each detail heading should be used for a separate descriptive paragraph. Allow them enough time in class to create one paragraph so they are able to ask questions before completing the assignment for homework. (See Student Worksheet 6— Semantic Map for Descriptive Article on page 68.)

Have students exchange papers with a partner. Each student will read his or her partner's paper and draw a picture to represent the bedroom described in the paper.

(continued)

LESSON 13 *(continued)*

Three students, Adam, Aaron, and Billy, wrote the following descriptive article about how one sixth-grade classroom participated in the planning for the school's 25th anniversary.

School gets new colors
by Adam, Aaron, & Billy

This fall Mrs. Spears and her sixth grade science class planted a wide variety of flowering trees, bushes, and other plants around the school. They did it to study plants and to make the school more beautiful for the 25th Anniversary.

Many parents and master gardeners helped figure out where to place the plants. The plants and equipment came from the teachers, the students, and their parents.

The money for the project came from the science budget, the fundraiser, and the 25th Anniversary Committee. The Zblewski Brothers donated six yards of black dirt and six yards of wood chips.

It took many hardworking people to finish this project. Keep an eye open in the spring for our school's new colors.

LESSON 14
Writing an Opinion Article
Janelle Legro and Jenny Wagner

Introduction

Persuasive writing is used to convince others to accept your views and beliefs. Students need to be able to see others' points of view, and students need to convince others of their views and beliefs. When writing an opinion article, it is important to follow these guidelines:

1. Begin by stating an opinion.

2. Include in the narrative three reasons why you have this opinion.

3. Give either a personal statement, prediction, or summary why you have this opinion at the end of the column.

Modeling

Persuasive writing involves three basic steps. Explain to students that first, you need to state your opinion on an issue. Next you need to state at least three concrete and convincing reasons to back up your opinion. Finally, conclude your article with a personal statement, prediction, or summary depending on what you want your audience to believe.

Construct an opinion paragraph using these criteria. Following is an example you can present to the class:

> Nike has the best athletic shoes on the market. (opinion)
> A famous basketball star is a spokesperson for the company. (reason 1)
> Our school basketball team wears Nike shoes. (reason 2)
> All of my best friends are wearing Nike shoes. (reason 3)
> This is why I believe all kids should wear Nike shoes. (personal statement)

Practice

Divide the class into groups of three. Provide each group with a sample situation or incident in which each student will take a role as participant. Each student will need to take on the beliefs of that role and convince others that their view is right. Then the group members will try to persuade the class to take their participant's view.

> Discuss the pros and cons of the school purchasing a new basketball hoop for the playground from the view of a student, the physical education teacher, and a member of the fundraising committee.

Give each group the graphic organizer for writing an opinion article and have students plot their articles. (See Student Worksheet 7—Mapping an Opinion Article on page 69.)

Chapter Five

Writing Different Types of Newspaper Stories

BY STUDYING the various types of articles included in the newspaper, students will learn that we can expand our world by learning about others and their reactions through the reporting of events that interest us. We learn about people and their experiences through human interest stories; we follow sports figures and their athletic contests through sports stories; we

discover diverse opinions through letters to the editor and book reviews. We learn what is important at any moment in time in our society—even if that society is as small as our school. These discoveries in the classroom provide the initiative to explore and understand larger communities—our city, state, country, and other countries.

There are different types of stories included in the newspaper. Feature stories can be divided into several types of articles. Categories of feature stories include

- personality sketches or profiles, which describe a person's flaws and good points; his or her appearance, mannerisms, characteristics, and

images; his or her successes and failures; the person's opinions, dreams, and ambitions (see Lesson 5 on page 23 for a student example of this type of feature);

- question-and-answer interviews provide word-for-word conversations between a reporter and a subject;

- narratives, which include first-person accounts or third-person re-creations of a dramatic situation, usually in chronological order;

- essays, which can be informative, opinionated, interpretive, inspirational, or humorous;

- exposés, which are nonfiction accounts that expose a

person or situation that has caused a problem;

- "how to" stories that tell what the problem is, then give step-by-step instructions on how to solve it, supplying all the basic steps and not assuming the reader is an expert;

- columns contain articles written in first person that express the writer's opinion; and

- reviews express opinions about a book, television show, movie, play, or musical event.

Good feature articles include people and quotes, statistics and description, such as colors, temperatures, smells, sizes, dimensions, sounds and noise levels, brightness or darkness, and textures. Similes and metaphors are used more in feature articles than in news stories.

Before writing a feature article, organize your ideas by brainstorming with others and researching the topic you want to cover. Decide what audience you are writing for, and determine the purpose of your story. This will give you an angle from which to write.

Summary

The newspaper contains information about various aspects of life in a community. Understanding the different types of articles that appear in a newspaper and the reasons why reporters write these stories broadens students' knowledge base for the various forms and purposes of written language. These understandings set the stage for using these literary forms and elements in any type of writing.

LESSON 15
Writing a Human Interest Story
Gretchen VanderLoop, Shana Hanson, and Angie Harrigan

Introduction

This lesson will teach students how to write a human interest story. Begin by explaining that a human interest story is about a special person, a special event, or a special place. Ask students to select a subject to write about from the following:

someone they know well or would like to know well;

a recent event or an upcoming event that they plan to attend; or

a place that has played an important role in their lives.

Next, have the students collect details by listing descriptions of their subject, remembering important things they have done, comparing their subject to other people, asking others about their subject, and explaining why their subject is important. Then, to answer the Five Ws, students should look at all the details related to their subject and decide why this person or event is worth sharing. For example, if a student is writing about a place, ask him to jot down what he hears, sees, smells, and feels when he visits that place, to remember personal experiences at that place, to compare it to other places, and to explain what he likes or dislikes about the place.

Explain that it is important to make the person, event, or action come alive for their readers.

Modeling

First, explain how to write a lead. The lead

is the first paragraph;

is 25 words or less;

tells what the story will be about;

hooks the reader; and

tries to answer the Five Ws (who, what, where, when, why) and One H (how).

Provide students with an example, and remind them that the most important information appears at the beginning and the least important information is at the end.

> Honest people returned $800 lost by shopper at East Town Grocery Store, this week.

(continued)

LESSON 15 *(continued)*

Now explain what comes next within the story. The writer would have to explain who the subject was, what happened specifically, how it happened, why it happened, and what happened because of it. Remember again that the most important information goes at the beginning and the least important information comes later.

Show the students the following example of a feature story:

> On Monday morning, Camila Shortings was shopping at Gordy's Food Market in the southern part of Little Chute. As time did not allow going to the bank, Camila put $800 into an envelope within her wallet. Sometime during her shopping the envelope fell out of her wallet.
>
> As Camila had approached the register she noticed it was gone. In a panic, she retraced her footsteps in the store, speaking with all of the employees en route.
>
> With little hope, Camila approached the service desk asking if someone had turned in an envelope with $800 cash in it. To Camila's great relief, the attendant said, "Yes, a young couple with three children turned it in." Camila searched the aisles for the family but, unfortunately, they had already left the store.
>
> Camila wanted this story to be printed in today's paper, in hopes that the family that found her money will see the article. She said she appreciates their good deed immensely.
>
> For the rest of us, let this be a reminder that there are still many honest, helpful people in the world.

Practice Divide the class into groups and decide which group will focus on a special place, person, or event. Students will then try to write their own human interest article using the methods introduced at the beginning of the lesson. Once the groups have completed rough copies of their articles, they will exchange with another group for editing and critiquing. Once the articles are polished, ask for volunteers to share their group's story.

The human interest article that follows was written by a group of fourth graders:

(continued)

County humane society offers winter pet care tips

by Kali, Amanda, Lacey, and Jessica

This article is about tips from the Portage County Humane Society for taking care of your pets in the winter, for our pets' safety.

If you have a cat, it should not be outside in the winter, says Kathy Simonis, education director at the animal shelter.

If a cat gets frostbite the body part that has frostbite will fall off. So, don't let your cat get frostbite, she says.

If you walk your dog in the winter, when you get home from walking the dog, put a warm cloth on its paws to get the salt and ice off. Otherwise, the dog feels like he is walking on tacks, she said.

Also, make sure you give your pet cold water two times a day so it does not freeze.

Try to keep your dog warm in the winter and make it happy every season.

Simonis said there are also a few things that a fourth grader can do for pets in the winter, such as donating these items to the shelter: chewies, tennis balls, old blankets, kitty toys, treats, bleach, and laundry soap for blankets and rugs.

The Portage County Humane Society gets about 50 calls a day from people, said Simonis. Sometimes there are as many as 60 animals at the shelter on one day. "For every person born, there are 15 dogs and 45 kittens born," she said.

That is why the people at the shelter cannot take all the animals home themselves, she said. This causes a problem sometimes, too, she said, because the workers sometimes fall in love with the animals and want to but can't take them all home.

If you'd like to work at the shelter, you must be 18, Simonis said. Workers clean the cages, feed and take care of the pets, try to find their owners, and play with the pets so they become used to people. "Also, you must be 18 to play with the animals," Simonis said.

LESSON 16
Writing a Sports Story
Ty Jury, Thad Schmitt, and David Juliot

Ty Jury, Thad Schmitt, and David Juliot

Introduction
Students read newspapers frequently, and they should be able to identify the various parts that make up an in-depth sports story. Sports stories recap the results of an athletic contest, profile an athlete's accomplishments, or address recreational activities. This lesson is designed to give students additional experience in the process of creating an effective sports story.

Continue the description of a sports story by explaining that the writer should provide a brief history of the opponents' records and include any unique facts about each team. Because there are many statistics available, it is important that the writer selectively incorporates them into the story and double-checks them for accuracy. Do the numbers add up? Caution students not to get carried away with statistics; some are more important than others.

Remind students to build the sports article using open-ended questions about what is happening and what is relevant, such as the objectivity (bias) of the information or the impact on the outcome of the game or players' performance.

Sports stories can be colorful, but are susceptible to clichés and jargon. Tell students to avoid this type of language if possible. Although writers should be cautioned of the overuse of clichés, usage of metaphors and similes is encouraged.

The sports reporter does not work for the team; he or she writes for the people, so objectivity is important. To write about a sport, one must understand that sport. Questions that a sportswriter should ask when writing an article include

Is the story fair/objective?

Does it show hero worship or promote the home team?

Modeling
Demonstrate a fictitious sports article in order to provide the students with an example of sports stories.

Bump, Set, Spike

McDill's fifth- and sixth-grade girls' volleyball team cruised to victory over its across-town rival, Jackson Elementary, 15-3 and 15-7.

The coach commented on the victorious team effort, "This is a big turnaround from last year's match when they beat us soundly. I was proud, today, of the girls' effort.

(continued)

LESSON 16 *(continued)*

Sally Lunt led McDill with 10 serving points, including four aces. Also for McDill, Beth Tubars chipped in with six assists. In a losing effort for Jackson, Rebacca Prellwitz contributed five scoring points.

The Lady Pickles will return to action next Tuesday when they host undefeated McKinley School at 4 p.m.

Practice

Circulate a collection of sports-action photographs from newspaper and magazine articles, allowing students to choose one. Students will make up all the information that is relevant for their sports story, such as team information and game statistics. Students will practice creating sports stories using their selections of photographs. While they are writing, help students to create their articles by asking the following questions:

Are you showing favoritism to either team?

Did your statistics add up and make sense?

Did you include the final score?

Will the reader understand the terms written in your story?

When students finish writing their sports stories, divide the class into groups. Allow each student to present to his or her group. After receiving feedback, students will continue to develop their sports stories until completed. Students will submit one story for teacher review and keep one to share with their group.

Three fourth graders wrote this sports article for their school newspaper:

Fourth graders play in the Super Bowl

by Billy, Adam, and Aaron

Most of the fourth graders play football at recess. We have four teams (out of 25 kids) with 6 kids on each team.

Every week one team plays the rest of the teams. Every week the captains change teams. We have a Super Bowl every Friday. Only the two top teams go to it.

For regular games we play by the baseball fields. For the Super Bowl, we use the big soccer field without the goals.

LESSON 17
Writing a Book Review
Angela Peters and Peggy Weigel

Introduction Share with students that this lesson will teach them how to write a book review for the newspaper. When reporters write a review, they read a book, watch a movie, or try a product, then report to the public about their findings. When writing this type of story, there are several guidelines to follow:

1. Grab the reader's attention.

2. Introduce the book, movie, or product.

3. When reviewing a book or movie, do not give away the ending.

4. Give enough information so the reader can decide whether to read the book, view the movie, or buy the product.

Modeling Bring in several children's books like *The Three Little Pigs* or *Cinderella* to model this process to the students. Brainstorm with the students for answers to the following questions, and document their answers on the board:

Who are the characters?

Where does the story take place?

What is the problem in the story?

Discuss how a reporter could get the reader's attention. Reviews can include the following aspects of a story: the beginning of the story, the problem in the story, or an introduction to a few interesting characters and how they are intertwined in the story. An example of using an interesting character for the review is illustrated here using the book *Charlotte's Web* by E.B. White (1952).

> Wilbur was to be butchered like all the other farm animals. He was tormented by the mere thought of it. He was special, he told all the other animals. The time drew nearer and nearer, but how could Wilbur save himself? His fate was in the hands of his best friend, Charlotte. She promised to help him, but she did not know how. What will become of Wilbur? Will Charlotte come to his rescue in time?

Practice Divide students into groups of three or four. Have them choose a book that they have all read or one they have been working on in class. They will write a book review together to present to their classmates. Have classmates give the other groups feedback on their reviews, especially in regards to clarity and attention-grabbing techniques.

(continued)

LESSON 17 *(continued)*

The following is a book review written for our classroom newspaper, *The Wildcat Gazette*:

What will Fudge do next?
by C.J. and Ashley

This awesome book is called "Tales of a Fourth Grade Nothing." This book is about two brothers, Peter, a fourth grader, and Fudge, 2, who are always getting in lots of trouble. The middle of the story is about their neighbors, "Mr. and Mrs. Juice," the Yarbys, who come over and sleep in Fudge's room. Well, Fudge wakes up and eats Peter's turtle, Dribble! To find out what other silly things Fudge does, you'll have to read this book!

The 120-page book, written by Judy Blume, was published in 1972 by Dell Publishing, a division of Bantam Doubleday-Dell Publishing Group Inc., New York.

LESSON 18
Writing a Letter to the Editor
Julie Trzebiatowski and Christina Bergman

Introduction

The opinion page—part of the editorial section of the newspaper—usually contains written materials that attempt to persuade or bring readers to the writer's side of an issue. Letters to the editor are a part of this section. They express an opinion of the reader regarding a certain subject. Today we will learn how to recognize and write this type of letter.

Modeling

Show a transparency of a news article. Then ask the students to write what they notice about the article, including who, what, where, when, why, and how. Discuss with students how news stories address specific events or topics.

Next, show a transparency of a letter to the editor, and ask students to write what they notice about the letter, such as a title, how the letter writer feels, the writer's name, and city. Discuss how these parts of this newspaper express subjective thoughts, feelings, and opinions of the writer and not the thoughts, feelings, and opinions of the newspaper.

Demonstrate how to write a letter to the editor, including the greeting, the body, and the salutation. Use a transparency of a letter to the editor for the class to read.

January 1, 2000

Dear Editor:

I feel that your article on dorm room decorating was very informative. My older brother is going to college next year and he is worried about the little room he has to live in. Your ideas will help his life be more fun.

Sincerely,
Johnny Appleseed

Practice

Give each student a newspaper to look at. Students will pick out an article that interests them. It may be a news, sports, feature, or editorial article. Ask students to compose their own letters to the editor regarding the articles they chose. The letters to the editor that they write will compose the open letter page of their newspaper. Ask for volunteers to share their chosen article and letter to the editor with the class.

Chapter Six

The Final Steps: Revision, Editing, Layout, and Publication

The Revision Process

STUDENTS HAVE collected information and drafted their articles. They should now be ready to refine their stories by sharing their writing with peer editors who will help them with the revision process. By actively participating in the revision stage of writing, students will become aware of the importance of this process in writing any text—reports, folk tales, mysteries, news articles, and poetry.

The Editing Process

In the days before personal computers, when copy was set into type letter-by-letter by the printer in the composing room, the type was set in a metal tray called a galley. Next, an inked impression, or a galley proof, was made. The machines that were used to set lines of type are no longer used today; they have been replaced by computers, which use electronic typesetting systems to create the words printed on the pages of a newspaper. Therefore nowadays the reporters and editors who use computers to type their news stories become the typesetters.

The copy editing process is the final process of editing the newspaper. This is when a proof, which is a page on which newly set copy is reproduced, is read for errors to be corrected. The editorial staff at the newspaper includes the copy editor and the proofreaders.

The copy editor improves the reporter's work by determining if it is grammatically correct; making sure it conforms to the stylebook;

checking for consistency and accuracy; and checking if the information is complete and objective. The copy editor also lays out the news stories and photographs in his or her section, and writes the headline for the stories and the cutlines for the photos.

The proofreader reads the news story before the final printing, marking any errors using the Editor's Checklist (see Student Worksheet 9). If the copy editor has done a good job, the proofreader will not need to mark many errors for correction.

Questions a reporter or copy editor should ask about every story include

Is everything spelled correctly?

Are the names spelled correctly?

Are the names, dates, numbers correct?

Are the commas in the right place?

Is the correct punctuation used throughout?

A good rule to follow during editing is keep things simple—don't clutter up a paragraph with unnecessary words when one will do.

Layout and Publication

Now that each article is ready to be published, all of the stories go to the editor. Deciding what to put in the paper is the role of the editor. Deciding how to organize the articles on the page, or the layout of the paper, is the role of the composing room staff. The people of the composing room work together to decide on what to include in the newspaper and where to put each article on the page.

Summary

Once they have completed the lessons in this chapter, students can sit back and wait for the publication to hit the newsstands. This is a time to be proud of their work and wait for the reactions of readers.

The Wildcat Gazette, created by Betsy Wiberg's fourth grade class, appears on the facing page.

The Wildcat Gazette

By Betsy Wiberg's 4th graders at Plover-Whiting Elementary
with UWSP students Mark K. Larson, Melissa Baran, Jenny Fox, Jenny Marx and Dan Nortman

County Humane Society offers winter pet care tips

Travis Gamboa

Kathy Simonis

Wildcat Gazette reporters

By Amanda Borski
Kali Brozik

Jessica Lang
Lacey Radomski

This article is about tips from the Portage Humane Society for taking care of your pets in the winter, for our pet's safety.

If you have a cat, it should not be outside in the winter, says Kathy Simonis, education director at the animal shelter.

If a cat gets frostbite the body part that has frostbite will fall off. So, don't let your cat get frostbite, she says.

If you walk your dog in the winter, when you get home from walking the dog put a warm cloth on its paws to get the salt and ice off. Otherwise, the dog feels like he is walking on tacks, she said.

Also, make sure you give your pet cold water two times a day so it does not freeze.

Try to keep your dog warm in the winter and make it happy every season.

Simonis said there are also a few things that a 4th grader can do for pets in the winter, such as donating these items to the shelter: chewies, tennis balls, bleach, old blankets, kitty toys, treats and laundry soap for blankets and rugs.

The Portage County Humane Society gets about 50 calls a day from people, said Simonis. Sometimes, there are as many as 60 animals at the shelter on one day.

"For every person born, there are 15 dogs and 45 kittens born," she said.

That is why the people at the shelter cannot take all the animals home themselves, she said. This causes a problem sometimes, too, she said, because the workers sometimes fall in love with the animals and want to but can't take them all home.

If you'd like to work at the shelter, you must be 18, Simonis said. Workers clean the cages, feed and take care of the pets, try to find their owners, and play with the pets so they become used to people.

"Also, you must be 18 to play with the animals," Simonis said.

Dolphins begin swim season

By Melissa Degen
Skott Schultz

The Stevens Point YMCA's Dolphins swim team last year's sectional champs, are at it again. All the coaches are very proud. The are doing a very good job getting them ready for this year's sectional meeting in the spring.

Jay Buckmaster, the head coach, says "the team will be bigger and stronger then ever." He also says he likes to motivate kids to do their best and to see them work hard.

Swimming is a great sport and Plover-Whiting Elementary hopes the Dolphins are successful again this year. Members of the team include Plover-Whiting Wildcat 4th graders Melissa Degen and Skott Schultz.

The season will lst until this spring. The team has meets almost every weekend and practices four or five times each week. Home team meets are at the Stevens Point YMCA.

Building additions proposed, need voter approval

By Jordan Hoerter

Andrew Keats
Cody Schmidt

We might be adding on to the school in the near future, because the kindergarten classrooms are too small...

"With all-day kindergarten we need more classroom...we just ran out of space," says Karen Martzahl a Plover-Whiting kindergarten teacher.

There is currently one kindergarten classroom on the second floor, and Martzahl's on the first floor. Expansion plans call for three smaller rooms to be added to the building, all together on the first floor along the north side, near Mrs. Stenstrom's 1st grade room.

Because there are also plans to widen Hoover Avenue on the building's west side, the school's main entrance was moved to the north side of the building, she said.

If you see the flagpole, that is where the new main doors are and will be located. Visitor parking will also be in this area.

The main office will be relocated into the area where the current band room is, off the main doors. The bigger band room will be a new room that is part of the addition.

A new, bigger music room is also in the plans.

Residents from Stevens Point and Plover will vote on a referendum for the changes, possibly during the April elections.

"If the voters say 'no, you cant' do it,' then we would have to have another plan," said Martzahl.

The costs for the proposed changes are still being determined, said Principal Bill King.

53

LESSON 19
Revising
Desiree Smolke and Jim Peterson

Introduction

Revision is the process of rearranging the story. In the revision process, the reporter might wish to substitute, delete, or rearrange the material in the article to make it more appealing to the reader. There are four types of revision that the reporter may wish to consider: additions, substitutions, deletions, and moves (Tompkins, 1998).

The students will learn the process of revision by working in small groups to revise rough drafts of news stories. Students can also be encouraged to use the computer for revising. Once the draft of a story has been revised, students may turn to their peers for reactions to their news stories.

Modeling

Introduce the students to this Revision Checklist:

- Did I begin my sentences in different ways?
- Did I write clear and complete sentences?
- Did I write sentences of different lengths?
- Did I use powerful verbs, specific nouns, and colorful modifiers?
- Did I use the correct word (to, two, or too; your or you're)?
- Is there anything the reader would want to know more about?
- Can I throw away any part?
- Do I need to add any details?
- Does my story have a distinct closing?
- Are my paragraphs in the right order (does my story flow)?
- Is the story complete?
- Does the story have a tight lead?
- Is the story accurate?
- Does the story have a powerful headline?

Show the students an example of a short story (three or four sentences) on the chalkboard or an overhead. Discuss with the students how the sentences could be revised using the checklist questions to make the story more understandable.

(continued)

LESSON 19 *(continued)*

I went to a football game.

I got a hot dog and a soda and a pretzel and went to my seat near the center of the field on the side where my favorite team's benches are but too far up in the stands to talk to the players or get any autographs. I thought the game was really cool because my favorite team won and the quarterback threw five touchdown passes and he is my favorite player. After the game I got to buy a T-shirt at a souvenir stand and I got a poster for my Grandpa because he couldn't come to the game with us.

Revision: I went to a football game with my dad. (More detail)

At the game, Dad bought me a hot dog, a soda, and a pretzel. (Correct punctuation)

My seat was near the center of the field. (Sentences of different lengths)

Now, help students to compare the paragraph that follows to the previous example. Use the Revision Checklist to help determine what revisions were made and why.

Revised story: I went to a football game with my dad. At the game, Dad bought me a hot dog, a soda, and a pretzel. My seat was near the center of the field. My favorite team's bench was right in front of me, but too far away for me to talk to the players or get their autographs. My team won the game, thanks to the quarterback's five touchdown passes. The quarterback is my favorite player. After the game I bought a T-shirt at the souvenir stand. I also got a poster for my grandpa, because he couldn't come to the game with us.

Practice

Put students in groups of three or four, and have them revise a short story. If stories written by students are not available, revise short newspaper stories by creating run-on sentences or rearranging sequence. (See Student Worksheets 8—Revision Checklist on page 70.) Place a transparency of the Checklist on the overhead for the class to refer to during the revision process. Ask students to present their revised stories to the class. Students should be able to refer to the checklist to explain why they made the changes they did.

LESSON 20

Editing

Amy Hartjes, Jenny Pritchard, and Kelly Seitz

Introduction   Explain to students that if others are to read what we have written, our written piece must be without spelling and punctuation errors, and the grammatical structures must be parallel. The person that checks for errors in writing is called a proofreader. Proofreaders use marks, identified on the Editing Checklist, when they edit a piece of writing. These marks are used to identify for the writer what type of error was made in the piece.

Modeling   Introduce the Editing Checklist to the students (see Student Worksheet 9 on page 71). Explain the marks on this checklist and how a proofreader marks errors on a piece of writing. Place a transparency of a paragraph containing poor grammar, spelling errors, and punctuation mistakes on the overhead. Ask the students if they see anything wrong with the paragraph shown. Using the Editing Checklist, discuss the importance of editing in the writing process.

President smith ran for office in the year 1999. he ran against sir william blake the current president.

Practice   Hand out the worksheet with the proofreader's marks to each of the students (see Student Worksheet 10—Practicing Editing on page 72). Using the marks, students will correct the sentences on the worksheet.

Once they understand what the marks mean, ask students to mark the news stories they have written using the Editing Checklist.

LESSON 21
Layout and Design
Jessica Hensley, Tammy L. Hole, Tony Gruber, and Leah Zietlow

Introduction Share with students that they are going to learn the layout and design process of creating a newspaper. Introduce the terms in Figure 6, which are used in the composing room.

Figure 6—Composing Room Vocabulary

Box: to put a ruled line around a story or picture. Generally, every photograph has a box around it.

Column: stories are arranged in columns, or lines going down the page.

Column inch: one inch of type (measured vertically), one column wide. Newspapers are measured in column inches. For example, the *Stevens Point Journal* uses a five-column format. A full page *SPJ* is five columns wide and 21 inches deep, or 105 column inches. A 22-page edition, therefore, has 22 pages, each with 105 column inches, so the total for the paper is 22 x 105, or 2,310 column inches.

Copy: all printed matter prepared for publication.

Cut: to shorten newspaper copy.

Deadline: time when all copy for an edition must be in, or when the press will start.

Dummy or map: diagram of a newspaper page used to show printers where stories, photos, and advertisements are to be placed.

Font or typeface: style of lettering used for type.

Layout: a plan showing the location of the stories, pictures, art, and ads on a page, done on a dummy sheet.

Paste-up: completed newspaper page ready to be photographed and printed.

Point size: a printer's measurement that indicates how tall a letter is. There are 72 points in an inch, so a headline in 72-point type has letters that are an inch tall. The point size that is used for headlines is generally between 24–48 points and boldface. Cutlines are written in italic, 10-point type. An article, however, generally uses 9-point type.

Put to bed: to send all copy to the presses to be printed.

Modeling Take an empty blueprint design and cut out articles and a photograph in order to design the newspaper to look like a finished product. Model how the articles and photograph will fit into the blueprint.

(continued)

L E S S O N 2 1 *(continued)*

Explain to students that the layout of the paper shows the location of the news stories, columns, and photographs. This layout is presented on what is called a *dummy*, which is a diagram that shows printers where to place these different elements of the paper. Terms students should be aware of for the layout and design are *jump* and *teaser*. Teaser is a short notice in the first page of a section telling about a story elsewhere in the paper, and a jump is a story that continues on a page of the newspaper other than where it started.

Discuss with students what types of articles they would like to include in their newspaper. Allow the class to design a dummy of the layout, illustrating the space that would be allowed for articles written by the reporters or reviewers. Students can use the Layout and Design Sheet in Appendix D, or they can create their own.

Practice

Give the students examples of newspapers, articles, photographs, and a dummy design. Have the students work in pairs or groups to cut down the articles and photos in order to design their own newspaper page. The students will then position their articles for their paper using the layout and design knowledge used throughout this lesson.

You can take photos of the students working on their newspaper. These photos could be used in their newspaper.

Chapter Seven

Student Evaluation of Unit Concepts

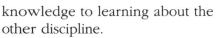

THE FINAL product, the newspaper, will be evaluated and critiqued by the intended audience. The newspaper, as Shanahan (1997) states, is an example of a "cultural way of communicating." Each discipline—anthropology, geology, zoology, journalism—has ways of communicating knowledge. As students become familiar with one discipline, they can apply this knowledge to learning about the other discipline.

Now students should be able to review all they learned about journalism in a fun and interesting way. This should be a time to play and celebrate the creation of their newspaper. This culminating activity is more of a celebration than a test. The terms and literary concepts included in this unit will be reviewed as students participate in a game.

LESSON 22

Evaluation of Newspaper Concepts

Jenny Fox, Erin Franck, and Liz Vinopal

Introduction Students will learn the terms and definitions associated with the newspaper—*news, columns, feature, reviews, lead, byline, headline, teaser, angle, jump, slug, beat, scoop, source, quote, dateline, assignment,* and *deadline.*

Modeling The class will participate in a game like the television game show *Jeopardy*. Create a grid with categories designated as Parts of a Newspaper, Newspaper Terms, and Reporter Terms at the top of the columns. Under each category, place point values from 100 to 600 in each box. Divide the class into teams, and give each team a bell to ring when they know the answer. The Game Master (teacher or student volunteer) gives a definition, and each team has to figure out what term fits the definition. As they think they know the answer, the team rings their bell. The first team to ring the bell gives the answer in the form of a question—"What is the lead?"

If their question fits the definition, the team selects a category and a point count for the next definition; the higher the point count, the harder the term. If a team does not ask the correct question, another team must ring the bell in order to give the correct question. If this team is correct, they can continue with the next question until they miss.

Explain the rules and then model a sample of the activity. For instance, read the definition of the word and instruct the students to say "What is..." and the term they think it is.

Teacher: "A mistake in the writing."
Reply: "What is a typo?"

Practice Ask students to participate in a round of the game. The categories will include parts of a newspaper, newspaper terms, and reporter terms. Figure 7 provides a point value and definition clue for words in each category. Give students a list of newspaper terms that may be included in the activity (see Figure 8 for a list of words).

Figure 7—Terms and Definitions for Game

Category—Parts of a Newspaper

100 Points: located on the first page of the newspaper; tells the paper's name, date of publication, and volume and issue numbers [Flag]

200 Points: the "title" of a newspaper story; summarizes the story [Headline]

(continued)

LESSON 22 *(continued)*

300 Points: the name of the writer at the beginning of an article [Byline]

400 Points: what a person says [Quote]

500 Points: the first sentence or paragraph of a story [Lead]

600 Points: caption under a photo or piece of artwork [Cutline]

Category—Newspaper Terms

100 Points: a current story, report, event, or problem [News]

200 Points: a story that summarizes the main ideas of an event, book, or movie [Review]

300 Points: article that contains opinions or is written in first person [Column]

400 Points: a story of general interest that is odd, unusual, or entertaining [Feature]

500 Points: to continue a story to another page [Jump]

600 Points: a short notice on the first page telling of a story somewhere else in the paper [Teaser]

Category—Reporter Terms

100 Points: a person or book that supplies the information of a story [Source]

200 Points: any job, duty, event, or story given to a reporter [Assignment]

300 Points: a time when everything is due [Deadline]

400 Points: an important story that the paper publishes before the competition does [Scoop]

500 Points: the area assigned to a reporter (school, police station, courthouse, etc.) [Beat]

600 Points: a story's main purpose [Angle]

Figure 8—Words That Could Be Used in a Game

(Words in italics are included with clues and point values in Figure 7.)

ad	comics	interview	publisher
angle	cutline	*jump*	*quote*
assignment	*dateline*	*lead*	*review*
banner	*deadline*	letters	*scoop*
beat	*editorial*	*news*	side bar
body	end mark	off the record	*slug*
box	*feature*	opinions	*source*
bullet	*flag*	photographer	sports
byline	*headline*	proof	*teaser*
column	inserts	proofreader	wire photo

Student Worksheet 1

News and Not News

Brainstorm with the members of your group to create five story ideas that would be news and five story ideas that would not be news. Write each of them under the correct column below.

News

1.

2.

3.

4.

5.

Not News

1.

2.

3.

4.

5.

Student Worksheet 2

People of the News

Using this semantic map, chart terms that are associated with each person who works at the newspaper.

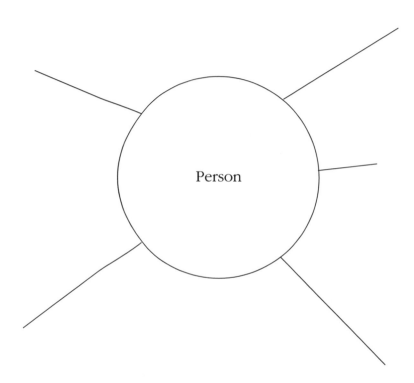

Student Worksheet 3

Sample Application for a Newspaper Position

Name: _____

Phone number: _____

Address: _____

Position applying for: _____

Qualifications: _____

_____

_____

_____

_____

_____

_____

Student Worksheet 4

Reporter Vocabulary Quiz

Name_____

Decide if the underlined words in the following sentences are used as part of reporters' vocabulary by comparing them to the Glossary of Newspaper Terms definitions. (These words are found in the miscellaneous section of the glossary.) If the words are used correctly, leave the lines below the sentence blank. If the words are not used correctly, write a new sentence on the lines using the glossary definition.

Example:
The reporter *beat* the eggs for breakfast.

The reporter's beat was the high school.

1. I'm going to *scoop* some ice cream.

_____

_____

2. John used the thesaurus as a *resource*.

_____

_____

3. Becky picked up her *one last check*.

_____

_____

4. The *hard news* was very entertaining.

_____

_____

5. The reporter's *assignment* was to cover the race.

_____

_____

6. It was an *objective* article because the reporter expressed her opinion.

_____

_____

7. The book had a blue *cover*.

_____

_____

8. The reporter made a *fact error* when he spelled a word wrong in his article.

_____

_____

Student Worksheet 5

Writing Lead Plus Equal Facts Articles

Fill in the boxes with your lead sentence and equal facts. Remember the lead sentence answers the questions *who, what, where, when, why,* and *how.* The three equal facts must support the lead sentence with information to help further explain the story.

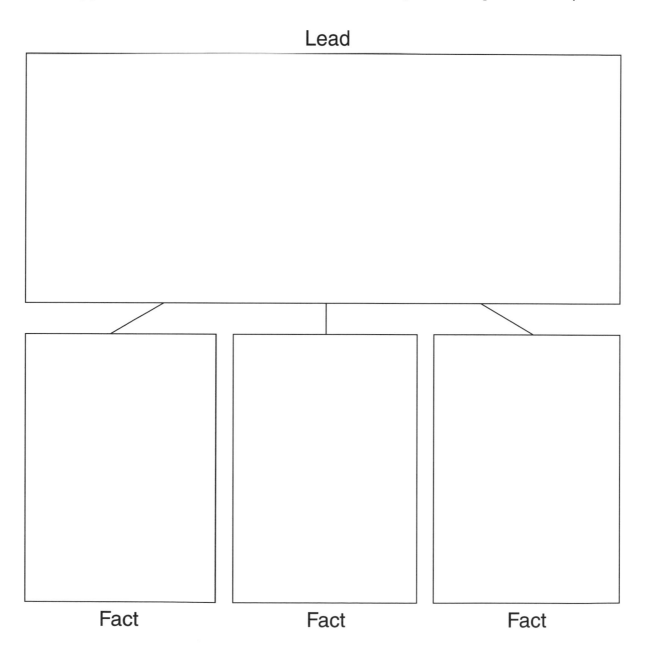

Lead

Fact   Fact   Fact

Student Worksheet 6

Semantic Map for Descriptive Article

Select at least three subtopics that you will use to describe your bedroom (e.g., color, furniture, size). Use one word (subtopic) per branch, adding more subtopics if needed. Create a list for each subtopic.

Description

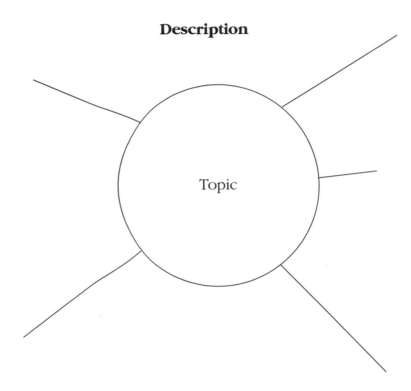

Student Worksheet 7

Mapping an Opinion Article

Plan your persuasive article using this Opinion Organizer and then write your opinion article.

OPINION

REASON 1	REASON 2	REASON 3

PERSONAL STATEMENT, PREDICTION, or SUMMARY

Student Worksheet 8

Revision Checklist

These are questions that you should ask yourself when reading a paper or article for revision. If you answer "no" to any of them, then you need to go back and make appropriate changes.

- Did I begin my sentences in different ways?

- Did I write clear and complete sentences?

- Did I write sentences of different lengths?

- Did I use powerful verbs, specific nouns, and colorful modifiers?

- Did I use the correct word (*to, two,* or *too; your* or *you're*)?

- Is there anything the reader would want to know more about?

- Can I throw away any part?

- Do I need to add any details?

- Does my story have a distinct closing?

- Are my paragraphs in the right order (does my story flow)?

- Is the story complete?

- Does the story have a tight lead?

- Is the story accurate?

- Does the story have a powerful headline?

Student Worksheet 9

Editing Checklist

Editor 1   Editor 2

Is the sentence clear and complete?

Is there correct punctuation at the end of sentences?

Are commas used properly?

Are all sentences started with a capital letter?

Are proper nouns capitalized?

Is the correct word used? example: *to, too, two*

Is spelling correct?

Are the apostrophes used correctly?

Signatures:

Editor 1_____

Editor 2_____

Student Worksheet 10

Practicing Editing

Using these marks, correct the following sentences:

Delete	ℓ	The small and tiny caterpillar crawled up the tree.
Insert	∧	Sammy called Austin and asked to come over.
Indent Paragraph	¶	Once upon a time there were three little pigs.
Capitalize	≡	I live in wisconsin.
Change to lower case	/	My Teacher is nice.
Add period	⊙	Mr. Smith mowed his lawn
Add comma	∧	I ate cookies pie and ice cream for my birthday.
Add apostrophe	⌄	I took Amys boyfriend to the movies.

All the dogs have their day: As moves go, this wasn't bad

By Jo Sandin
of the *Journal Sentinel* staff

Now it's a humane society.

Even though the new brick building at 4500 W. Wisconsin Ave. won't open as the Wisconsin Humane Society until Wednesday, and it will take far longer than that for staff members to unpack their files, the place already is firmly in the possession of the most important residents—280 cats, more than 40 dogs, about 50 gerbils, hamsters, rabbits and the occasional raccoon.

Cats were introduced to their new temporary home last week.

Dog Moving Day on Monday proceeded to a cacophony of woofs, arfs, yips, and whines.

A face-licking, tail-wagging, leash-yanking, floor-sniffing, yelp-raising good time was had by all.

All day, Kim Schlote and Heather Seidel, animal adoption counselors at the society, shuttled between the dingy old shelter at 4151 N. Humboldt Ave. and the

bright new building. Their vehicle, a gleaming white truck with separate compartments for seven dogs, eventually will be used as a mobile adoption van taking animals in search of new homes.

Coaxing a male beagle—still nameless—into the van was an adventure. Displaying every bit of his tracking ancestry, he had picked up all kinds of interesting scents and wanted to follow each one.

From his wire enclosure in a corridor dim with age and wear, a Labrador-Dalmatian mix named Bo leaped into Schlote's embrace and onto a leash. Sophie, a tan and white boxer mix, thought Seidel deserved a doggie kiss for letting her out, but she just didn't want to walk up the steel ramp into the truck.

While Schlote gathered the big dog into her arms and boosted her

---

Reprinted with permission from the *Milwaukee Journal Sentinel* (November 30, 1999).

into the van, the other dogs sounded a chorus of greetings.

Inside the driver's compartment, however, the canine commentary on the ride was muted.

The same is true of the sound level inside the new building. Sounds are softened. So are smells, thanks to an air circulation system designed for maximum health benefits.

Here, each dog has a separate room— large enough to entertain prospective adoptive owners. Sunlight from big windows in a common area streams through window and door glass into each room, where each dog can curl up on his own fluffy bed.

The dogs wouldn't want to live there, but it's a really nice place to visit.

Dorm room decorating all about making the most of limited space

They may look like typical dorm rooms—containing desks, dressers, TVs, beds—but how University of Wisconsin–Stevens Point students design and decorate their home away from home varies widely.

Sophomore Brooks Nimmer has fake ivy climbing along a shelf connecting the top portion of the two desks and strands of white Christmas lights hanging in her Hyer Hall room.

Justin Gerlach, also a sophomore, has photos of his friends—both from back home in New London and new ones he's made here—tacked up around his room in Baldwin Hall.

And Nick Weno's Smith Hall room has just about everything: a double-wide dresser, computer, refrigerator and microwave, and an entertainment center.

"We just got down here the first day and moved stuff around for about a week," said Wenos, a sophomore who hails from Rhinelander.

"Eventually we got it the way we want it," he said. It helps that he and roommate Jeff Burkhardt,

also of Rhinelander, have a lounge room, which is about 3 feet wider than (though the same depth as) other dormitory rooms found on campus.

The little bit of extra space amounts to a lot for the two students. They were able to fit a full-sized couch and a loveseat in their room.

Despite the smaller-sized rooms, many students are still finding a bit of extra space for parties, homework sessions or just hanging out.

How? By lofting. That is, rigging one or both beds up off the floor in order to fit items underneath. It's standard practice now, according to residence hall directors, and some students even get their parents involved.

But really, there's nothing fancy to it, said Jessica Schmidt, a sophomore who resides in Smith Hall.

"You just try to get everything to fit that you want basically," she said. "Everybody does it a little different."

Like Wenos and Burkhardt, Schmidt's room has both beds loft-

---

ed. Gerlach, who has a single room, has lofted one bed and the other slid in a sort of "T" shape underneath it.

Nimmer chose the bunked-type option in which one bed is lofted and the other lined up parallel under it. On the opposite side, there is a loveseat/hide-a-bed couch for guests.

"Everybody comes in here and says, 'Oh, it looks like home,' but we figure if you don't add your own touch… You want to give it something you want to come back to at the end of the day," Nimmer said.

Another popular decor for dorm rooms are futons and related furniture items, like papazan chairs.

But it's not just the furniture that makes the dorm room a second home.

"I like to be outdoors, I like nature," Gerlach said, explaining why so many nature-themed pictures and posters hang on the walls of his room.

"That's when I can relax the most and when I have those up and I can zone out, it's relaxing."

The poster scene varies as much as the decorating style.

There are animals, athletic events or star athletes, favorite bands or musicians, women in bikinis or men in Speedos.

Add to that scheme sports paraphernalia, perhaps some plants, a computer, an entertainment center complete with mid-sized screen TVs, video cassette recorders, stereos and speakers, lamps and maybe your own carpeting (even though some rooms come with carpet already in them) and you've got yourself a pretty livable pad.

Some students will spill the decorating onto the door with a notepad, photos, postcards, arts or crafts.

And a few will embellish by putting items like glow-in-the-dark stars on the ceiling (nothing hanging as that would be a fire hazard, hall directors say).

Really, whatever makes students feel comfortable—that's the ticket.

"You're in here for quite a long time," Wenos said. "It's not a real big space and you're living with someone else so you want to be comfortable—unless you study all the time, which most people don't."

Layout and Design Sheet

Page 1

Title Plate (Flag)		
News Story		Photo
News Story	News Story	Human Interest Story

Page 2

Letter to the Editor	News Story	Book/Movie Review
Human Interest Story	Photo	Sports Story

Glossary of Newspaper Terms

Departments and people; sections of the newspaper; types of stories

Ad manager: the person who oversees the ad representatives, who sell advertising space to companies.

Advertisement: a message, also called an ad, which sells something in space paid for by a company or organization.

Classified advertising: also called "want ads." These are usually short ads placed by the public bought by the word or by the line.

Column: articles that contain opinions or are written in first-person.

Copy editor: the person who checks the entire story for accuracy to see that there are no factual, spelling, or grammatical errors in it. He or she also rewrites, revises, and corrects any errors in the story if needed, and writes a headline for it.

Display advertising: ads that usually have pictures and prices to advertise stores, foods, and services. See *advertisement.*

Editor in chief: the person who is in charge of deciding what news goes into the paper. He supervises the section editors, their reporters, and the copy editors.

Editorial: an article expressing the opinion of the newspaper regarding a certain subject. These are persuasive stories or columns. News stories should not be editorialized.

Editorial cartoon: art that expresses an opinion about a current issue or event, usually found in the opinion/editorial section.

Feature: a story usually about a subject that is not late-breaking news but is of general interest, is odd or unusual, or is entertaining. This type of story is less formal than a straight news story.

Flag: the name and logo of the newspaper that runs at the top of the front page.

Front page: the first page of a newspaper, which contains the most important stories of the day.

Graphs/charts: information used to support a story without bogging down the story with data.

Index: listings of sections usually found on the front page.

Inserts: supplements, usually folded inside the regular paper.

Letter to the editor: a letter written by a reader to express an opinion on a topic or event reported in the newspaper.

Managing editor: usually the second in command, behind the editor in chief.

Masthead: the detailed information printed in the newspaper stating the title, address, ownership, and subscription rates.

News editor: the person in charge of determining what stories are newsworthy; he or she assigns stories to reporters.

News story: a media report presenting new information, especially recent events in the community, in a straightforward and concise manner. The information in a news story should be objective and accurate.

Obituary: a death notice or short biographical account of someone's life, including information about funeral arrangements and services. Called "obit" for short.

Opinion page: these feature subjective thoughts, feelings, and opinions of newspaper's readers.

Photographer: a person who takes a picture to illustrate a story. Sometimes the picture stands alone without a story. This is called a *feature* or *news photo*, depending on its content.

Proofreader: one who reads the proof pages and marks errors for correction.

Publisher: head of a newspaper who oversees business operations.

Reporter: person who is assigned to cover a story; he or she gathers information by attending an event, doing research, and interviewing those involved, then writes a story that tells readers what happened, answering the Five Ws and One H.

Review: a column expressing an opinion about a book, television show, movie, play, or musical event.

Teaser: a short notice usually in the first page of a section telling about a story of interest elsewhere in the paper.

Parts of a Newspaper Story

Angle: the reason a reporter is writing a story, why it is significant, important, or interesting—what the reporter's main point is. It is also called a *news peg*.

Associated Press (AP): a news-gathering agency serving many newspapers. Correspondents around the world write stories that are transmitted to be printed in newspapers that subscribe to the service.

Banner: a headline running across the top of the entire front page.

Body: the main part of the story, after the lead.

Bullet: a large black dot used at the left edge of a column to mark each item in a series.

Byline: the name of the writer or writers (and their roles with the paper) appearing at the head of a news story or along a photograph.

Clip art: generic artwork that is used to illustrate a story in place of a chart or photograph.

Cutline/caption: explanatory information under a photo or piece of art.

Dateline: words at the beginning of a story that tells the location and/or date of origin of the story. Datelines are not used for local stories.

End mark: the symbol at the end of a reporter's story to indicate the end of the piece. Generally the symbol is either ### or -30-

Headline: the boldface phrase that appears before a story, also called a *head*. It summarizes the story's main point.

Illustration: artwork, clip art, charts, or photographs that enhance a story's content.

Inverted pyramid: form for a news story in which facts are arranged in descending order of importance; the story is summarized and then supported by the minor facts.

Jump: to continue a story to another page.

Lead: the first paragraph that gives the story's main facts; the most important sentence of the story.

Localize: to give a story a local angle or twist so it captures the interests of the local readers.

Photograph: a picture that accompanies a story or stands by itself; can also be used to illustrate an ad.

Side bar: a short story that is about the same general subject as a longer story and is placed on the page in a way that shows the reader that the two stories are related. Secondary information and details are often contained in a sidebar, which is often boxed.

Slug: a two- or three-word identification used at the top of the news story to suggest what it is about.

Quote: what a person said, directly or indirectly. A direct quote is the speaker's exact words, verbatim, enclosed in quotation marks. Indirect quotes paraphrase what was said by the person.

The Five Ws and One H: The basic questions that a story must answer—who, what, where, when, why, and how.

Wirephoto: a photograph transmitted by telephonic or telegraphic equipment.

Production Terms

Box: to put a line around a story or picture. Generally, every photograph has a box around it.

Column: stories are arranged in columns or lines going down the page.

Column inch: one inch of type (measured vertically), one column wide. Newspapers are measured in column inches.

Composing room: where copy, headlines, and artwork are put together for printing.

Copy: all printed matter prepared for printing.

Cut: to shorten newspaper copy.

Deadline: a time at which all copy for an edition must be in.

Dummy: a diagram of a newspaper page used to show printers where stories, pictures, and ads are to be placed.

Font/typeface: the style of lettering used for type.

Layout: a plan showing the location of the stories, pictures, art, and ads on a page, done on a dummy sheet.

Paste-up: a completed newspaper page ready to be photographed and printed.

Proof: a page on which newly set copy is reproduced to make it possible to read for errors to be corrected.

Point size: measurement that indicates how tall a letter is. There are 72 points in an inch. The point size that is used for headlines is generally between 24 and 48 points, boldface, while cutlines are written in 10-point italic type. An article, however, generally is printed in 9-point type.

Put to bed: to send the paper to the presses to be printed.

Rough draft: a copy of a story before it has been revised.

Stop the press!: What the editor in chief yells if there is a late-breaking story that has just occurred, or a story that has just been updated and needs to be fixed. An example would be if you learn the President has just been shot and his condition has just changed. Only the most important of all important stories deserves this command because it is very costly to stop production.

Miscellaneous Terms

Accuracy: The rule of journalism. Always check facts.

AP Stylebook: the stylebook created by the Associated Press and used by most newspapers; it contains the accepted rules regarding style for punctuation, use of numbers, capitalization, and other features of the written language.

Article: another word for a story.

Assignment: any job, duty, or event given to a reporter to write about.

Attribution: the source of information or facts contained in a story. To give attribution means to recognize the source, which could be a person (such as the police chief, CEO, manager, or witness), or a document that supplied this information. Numbers and statistics should always be attributed. The How, Why, and any opinions in a story should also be attributed be-cause this ensures credibility if the source is reputable and accurate, and it allows the reporter to keep his or her objectivity without being the source or expert.

Beat: the area assigned to a reporter for his or her regular coverage, such as the courthouse, the schools, or the police station.

Circulation: the number of papers printed by a newspaper each day. Also, the name of the newspaper department that delivers and sells papers.

Cover: to get all the facts of a news event and write about the event in a story.

Fact error: this means the reporter spelled something wrong or supplied information that was incorrect in his or her story. He or she was inaccurate.

Hard news: difficult news that is hard to digest and sometimes dull, such as political stories. It is straight news, meant to inform. *Soft news*, such as a feature story, moves the reader and generates an emotional response. It is meant to entertain.

Interview: the process used by a reporter to ask a source questions to find out answers for the Five Ws and One H for a story.

Journalism: the trade, technique, or profession used by those on a newspaper staff to report and publish the news for the public to read.

Libel: injury to reputation or defamation of character that appears in print; can be words, pictures, or cartoons that expose a person to public hatred, shame, disgrace, or ridicule.

Listen: what every good reporter does when interviewing someone and taking notes.

Objective: what every good reporter wants to be when writing a news story. Use concrete facts, such as 6'11", 12 lights, or peas, instead of personal interpretations such as tall, well-lit, or nauseating greens.

Off the record: what is agreed to when a source supplies information that he or she does not want to be used in a story, or does not want to be quoted. However, you are given the information, you must keep his or her name secret, and try to verify it from another source.

Press release: information supplied by a company's public relations department to offer its position or accounts of a story, event, or accomplishment by the company or its personnel.

Resources: anything a reporter uses to make the job easier, such as a dictionary, stylebook, thesaurus, or official document.

Scoop: an important story that a newspaper publishes before its competition does.

Source: a person, book, or document that supplies the information used in a story. This is who or what the reporter attributes that information to.

Strunk and White: authors of the book *Elements of Style*, which is a must-read for a good reporter. It contains all the basic English material you need to know about writing well.

Typo: short for a *typographical error.*

Wire services: news-gathering agencies, such as the Associated Press.

Stylebook

THE STYLEBOOK dictates writing practices and word usage (such as punctuation, capitalization, spelling, abbreviations, addresses, and dates) in a story to ensure that consistency and uniformity occur throughout a paper. These basic rules are taken from the most frequently used style tips from the *Associated Press Stylebook and Libel Manual* (1998).

abbreviations: abbreviate the titles *Dr., Gov., Mr., Mrs., Rep.,* and *Sen.* when used before a full name outside of direct quotations. Spell out all titles, except *Dr., Mr.* and *Mrs.*, when they are used before a name in direct quotations. Abbreviate *junior* or *senior* after an individual's name to *Jr.* or *Sr.: Ken Griffey Jr.* Abbreviate *company* (co.), *corporation* (corp.), *incorporation* (inc.), and *limited* (ltd.) when they are used after the name of a corporate entity.

accept, except: accept means to receive; except means to exclude.

addresses: Abbreviate and capitalize *avenue* (Ave.), *boulevard* (Blvd.), and *street* (St.), in numbered addresses: *He lives at 1600 Pennsylvania Ave.; He lives on Pennsylvania Avenue.* Similar words such as *alley, drive, road,* and *terrace* are always spelled out and capitalized when used with an address. Always use figures for an address number: *9 Morningside Circle.* Spell out and capitalize *first* through *ninth* when used as street names, such as *77 Fifth Ave.*, but use figures with letters for *10th* and above, such as *100 21st St.* Abbreviate compass points when used in a numbered address, such as *222 E. 42nd St.*

affect, effect: *affect* as a verb means to influence; *effect* as a noun means a result.

ages: always use figures. Examples: *An 8-year-old boy. The boy is 6 years old. The boy, 9, has a sister, 10. The woman, 22, has a daughter 4* *months old. The law is 8 years old. The woman is in her 70s.* (note no apostrophe)

all right: never *alright*.

all time, all-time: An *all-time* high, but the greatest runner of *all time*.

a.m., p.m.: lowercase, with periods. Avoid the redundant *9 a.m. this morning*.

ampersand (&): used only when part of a company's formal name, such as *Baltimore & Ohio Railroad* or *Newport News Shipbuilding & Dry Dock Co.* The ampersand should not otherwise be used in place of *and*.

apostrophe: used for omitted figures, such as the *class of '81*, or *the '50s*.

athletic teams: capitalize teams, associations and recognized nicknames: *the Packers, the Big Ten, the A's, the Orioles*.

blond, blonde: use *blond* as a noun for males, *blonde* as a noun for females, but *blond* as the adjective for all applications, such as *She has blond hair. Brunet* and *brunette* work the same way.

cents: spell out the word *cents* and lowercase, using numerals for amounts less than a dollar, such as *7 cents, 24 cents*. Use a $ and decimal system for larger amounts, such as $1.01 or $13.48.

city: capitalize *city* when it is part of a proper name, such as *Kansas City* or *New York City*, but not other times, such as *a Wisconsin city, the city of Stevens Point, the city police department*.

collective nouns: nouns that denote a unit take singular verbs and pronouns, such as *class, committee, crowd, family, group, herd, jury, orchestra, team*. Examples: *The committee is meeting to set its agenda. The jury reached its verdict. The team won its game*.

company: use *Co.* or *Cos.* when a business uses either word at the end of its proper name, such as *Ford Motor Co.*, but *Aluminum Company of America. Ford Motor Co.'s profits were down*.

composition titles: for book, play, movie, song, poem and television program titles, and titles of lectures, speeches or works of art, follow these guidelines: Capitalize the principal words, including prepositions and conjunctions, of four or more letters; capitalize the words *the, a, an*, and a word of fewer than four letters if it is the first or last word of a title, put quotation marks around the titles, except for books that are considered reference material, which should be italicized. Examples: "Gone With the Wind," "Of Mice and Men," "The Rise and Fall of the Third Reich," "Happy Days," *World Book Encyclopedia*.

contractions: do not use contractions (*don't, isn't, can't*) in a story unless they are part of a direct quote.

corporation: abbreviate *Corp.* when a company uses the word at the end of its name, such as the *Copps Corp.* Spell it out and lowercase when corporation stands alone.

county: capitalize when it is part of a proper name, such as *Portage County*, but lowercase plural combinations, such as *Portage and Waupaca counties*.

courtesy titles: in general, *Mr., Mrs., Miss* or *Ms.* are not used on the first reference. Instead, identify the person by first and last name, such as *Joe Smith* and *Josephine Smith*. On second reference, use *Mrs.* or *Miss Smith* if it is needed to distinguish between Mr. and Mrs. Smith.

days of the week: capitalize, but do not abbreviate the days of the week.

decades: use numerals to indicate decades of history. Use an apostrophe to indicate numerals that are left out. Show plural by adding *s* without the apostrophe: the 1950s, the '80s, the mid-1970s.

department: lowercase *department* when it stands alone or when plural, but do not abbreviate it in any usage. Capitalize it if it is part of a specific title, such as *Department of Transportation*.

dimensions: spell out *inches, feet, yards,* and use figures to indicate depth, height, width, and length, such as *she is 5 feet 2 inches tall, the 5-foot-two woman, the 3-by-4 box, the box is 3 feet by 4 feet*.

distances: spell out *one* through *nine*, but use figures for *10* and above, such as *Becca walked five miles, but Mark walked 12*.

doctor: use *Dr.* on first reference for those who hold a doctor of medicine degree, *physicians such as Dr. Jonas Salk*.

dollars: use figures and the *$* sign, such as *The sandwich cost $3.99.* For amounts more than $1 million, use the $ sign and numerals up to two decimals, such as *$6.72 million*, unless it needs to be specific, such as *$6,721,999*.

each: takes a singular verb.

ensure, insure: *ensure* means to guarantee; *insure* refers to insurance.

Fahrenheit: The temperature scale commonly used in the U.S. (note the space and no period after the *F*). Use a number and letter (without a period), such as *55 F*).

family names: capitalize words that tell family relationships when they precede the name of a person such as *Grandfather Hansen*, or when they are a substitute for a person's name such as *I gave Mother a present*.

firefighter: not *fireman*, and *police officer*, not *policeman*.

food names: capitalize brand names and trademarks, but most food names are lower case: Tabasco sauce, Hatfield ham; apples, cheese, peanut butter.

fort: do not abbreviate for cities or military installations, such as *Fort McCoy* or *Fort Lauderdale*.

fractions: spell out amounts less than *one* in stories, using hyphens between the words, such as *two-thirds, one-half*, and use figures for precise amounts larger than one, converting to a decimal if practical, such as *19.7*.

girlfriend, boyfriend: one word each, not two.

goodbye: not *goodby*.

grade, grader: hyphenate the noun and adjective forms, such as *first-grader* or *10th grader*, or the *first-grade student, the 12th-grade student*.

holidays: capitalize, such as *New Year's Eve, Christmas, Halloween*.

in, into: *in* indicates location, such as *Becca was in the kitchen. Into* indicates motion, such as *Becca walked into the kitchen*.

incorporated: if part of a corporate name, abbreviate and capitalize as *Inc.*

initials: use periods and no space when an individual uses initials instead of a first name, such as *H.L. Mencken*.

injuries: they are *suffered* or *sustained*, not *received*.

innocent: use *innocent* rather than *not guilty*, in describing a jury verdict or a defendant's plea, to guard against the word *not* being inadvertently dropped.

it's, its: *it's* is a contraction for *it is; its* is a possessive pronoun, such as *The team lost its game*.

jargon: language specific to a trade, profession, class or fellowship; it is generally to be avoided, as is the use of slang, expletives, profanity, and obscenity. Also avoid language that is racial or creates sexual stereotypes, or represents a euphemism, colloquialism or provincialism. Also, avoid using clichés.

left hand (noun), **left-handed** (adjective), **left-hander** (noun).

magazine names: capitalize the name, but do not put quotes around it. Also, lowercase *magazine* unless it is part of the actual title—*Sports Illustrated, Harper's Magazine, Time Magazine.*

mailman: *letter carrier* is preferred because many women hold this job.

media: this word is plural, when it refers to newspapers, radio, television.

months: capitalize the names of all months in all uses. When used with a specific date, these months are abbreviated: *Jan., Feb., Aug., Sept., Oct., Nov.,* and *Dec.* Otherwise, spell out when using the month alone, or with a year alone. Do not separate the month and year with a comma: *January 1973 was a cold month.* If a month, day, and year are used, set the year off with commas: *On Feb. 14, 1999, Mark and Becca are going to get married.*

nicknames: use a nickname only if the person prefers to use that name in place of a given name: *Duke Snider.* If a nickname is used within a person's full name, set it off by using quotation marks: *Sen. Henry "Scoop" Jackson.*

OK, OK'd, OK'ing, OKs: do not use *okay.*

percentages: use figures: *3 percent, 45.7 percent, 19 percent.* Use *percent* with each figure.

persons: do not use words such as *chairperson* or *spokesperson.* Instead, use *chairman* or *chairwoman,* or *spokesman* or *spokeswoman.*

president: capitalize when used as a formal title before a name: *President Clin-*ton, *President Bush.* Lowercase in all other uses: *He is running for president.*

principal, principle: a *principal* runs a school or is something of primary importance; a principle is a fundamental truth, law, doctrine or motivating force.

quotation marks: open-quotes (") and close quote (") marks are used to set off the direct words of a speaker: *"I did not take the car to the store," he said. "I did not buy any apples," he said, "because one of them looked rotten." He said, "I did not go to the store to buy some apples." He said he did not buy any apples because "one of them looked like it was rotten."* When a paragraph ends with a quote that continues into the next paragraph, do not put quotation marks at the end of the sentence in the first paragraph, but begin the second paragraph with quotes: *He said, "I am not going to run for president this year because I want to spend more time with my family.*

"However, I think my successor, Vice President Stevens, deserves to continue our platform. He will make a worthy candidate, one who can carry it out."

ratios: use figures and a hyphen: *He won by a 2-to-1 vote, a 3-1 ratio.*

river: capitalize when it is part of a proper name: *Mississippi River.* Lowercase in other cases *the Wisconsin and Mississippi rivers; The river winds through the state.*

saint: abbreviate as *St.* when used in the names of cities, saints and other places: *St. Louis, St. John, St. Lawrence Seaway.*

scores: use figures exclusively, using a hyphen between the totals: *The Brewers defeated the Cubs, 7-6. The Packers beat the Bears, 42-21.*

seasons: lowercase *winter, spring, summer,* and *fall* unless part of a formal name: *Winter Carnival, Summer Olympics.*

second reference: acronyms are acceptable for second references; spell out the name on first reference: *Federal Communications Commission,* then *FCC.* The first time a person is named in a story, use a first and last name. On second reference, using only the last name is sufficient, unless the name is shared by more than one person mentioned in the story: *James Edwards said... Edwards said.* Also, remember that a person should be identified correctly; spell the name correctly, too. If need be, ask for the correct spelling, or verify it by checking the appropriate reference materials.

state names: spell out the name when a state stands alone in a story. Abbreviate the states as follows, when used with a city: *Ala., Ariz., Ark., Calif., Colo., Conn., Del., Fla., Ga., Ill., Ind., Kan., Ky., La., Md., Mass., Mich., Minn., Miss., Mo., Mont., Neb., Nev., N.H., N.J., N.M., N.Y., N.C., N.D., Okla., Ore., Pa., R.I., S.C., S.D., Tenn., Vt., Va., Wash., W. Va., Wis., Wyo.* Eight states are never abbreviated: *Alaska, Hawaii, Idaho, Iowa, Maine, Ohio, Texas,* and *Utah.* Place a comma between the city and the state, and another comma after the state: *He was going from Eau Claire, Wis., to Louisville, Ky., to see his horse race.*

temperatures: use figures except for zero: *The temperature at noon was 32. The low was minus 6,* or *The low was 6 below zero.*

their, there, they're: *their* is a possessive pronoun: *Becca and Mark went to their house. There* is an adverb indicating direction: *They went there for dinner.*

They're is a contraction for *they are: They're coming home soon.*

time element: use *Monday, Tuesday* etc., for days of the week within seven days before or after the date of publication. Use the month and figure for dates beyond this range. Use *today, this morning, tonight,* as appropriate for afternoon editions.

times: use figures except for *noon* or *midnight: 10 a.m., 3:33 p.m.* Avoid redundancies such as *10:31 a.m. this morning* or *9 p.m. Monday night.*

TV: can be used as an adjective: cable TV. Otherwise, use television.

United States: spell out as a noun; use *U.S.* only when it is used as an adjective: *We went to the United States. We went to see the U.S. Court of Appeals.*

vice: use two words for positions, without a hyphen: vice president.

war: capitalize when used as part of the name for a specific conflict: *Vietnam War, World War II,* the *Korean War.*

who's, whose: *who's* is a contraction for who is: *I do not know who's at the door. Whose* shows possession: I do not know whose bike that is.

years: use figures, without commas: 1981. Use an s without an apostrophe to indicate spans of decades or centuries: the 1950s, the 1700s.

yesterday: use only in direct quotes; otherwise use the day of the week.

youth: boys and girls ages 13–18; those 18+ are referred to as a man or woman.

ZIP codes: use all capitals for ZIP but lowercase code. Run the five digits together without a comma. Do not put a comma between the state name and the ZIP code: New York, NY 10020.

Additional Resources

Student Writing

Childrens Express Worldwide (CE)
http://www.cenews.org
Childrens Express Worldwide is an international news network for young students ages 8–18 who write news articles from a student's perspective. Articles are about current news and issues that affect young citizens. CE is a free service and reporters work in collaboration with teenage editors.

CRAYON
http://www.crayon.net
CRAYON stands for CreAte Your Own Newspaper. This site provides a vehicle for students to create a free online newspaper. Using the templates, students can add links from lists of regional, national, and international news sites. There also are samples of student newspapers online. Student newspapers can be updated. This site also includes links to newspapers in the U.S. (by state), Canada, and the world.

Daryl Cagle's Professional Cartoonists Index
http://www.cagle.com
This site is maintained by Daryl Cagle, Vice President of the National Cartoonists Society. Included in this site is an extensive collection of editorial cartoons, plus teachers' guides for lesson plans for elementary (grades 3–5), middle school, and high school students who want to study and create cartoons.

Kidnews

http://www.kidnews.com

This is a safe site for students to read and submit news stories with students from around the world on a wide variety of topics. In addition, students can express their own opinions and views on different topics. Stories are edited for content and language before they are posted. This site also includes collaborative projects between classrooms.

National Elementary Schools Press Association (NESPA)

http://www.nespa.org

This site is sponsored by NESPA, which is an organization dedicated to helping elementary and middle school students develop a class or school newspaper.

News Sources for Children

Infoplease

http://www.infoplease.com/

Infoplease is sponsored by the Family Education Network and is an almanac for kids that offers a brief history of journalism and the newspaper. The Daily Almanac and the Breaking News sections are particularly interesting. This site also includes links to other sites related to newspapers and news periodicals.

News Directory

http://www.news.com

This site is a guide to English-language media online. This site provides over 17,000 categorized links to newspapers by country and region (including Africa, Asia, Europe, North America, Oceania, and South America), and mag-

azines by subject (including arts & entertainment, business, health, sports).

New York Times

http://www.nyt.com

This site provides daily national and international news from the *New York Times*. Students can read about topics such as science/health, sports, weather, and books.

Scholastic News

http://teacher.scholastic.com/newszone/index.asp

This news site for children is nicely organized for students to check on breaking news. Today's top stories are just a click away.

Weekly Reader Galaxy

http://www.weeklyreader.com

This site is sponsored by the *Weekly Reader* and is designed for children, parents, and teachers by grade levels. Students can read about current events and press releases.

The WIRE—News from the Associated Press

http://wire.ap.org

Students can use this site sponsored by the Associated Press to search news by regions and states. Local news from selected newspapers is listed by regions in the U.S., and a drop-down menu identifies specific cities.

4News

http://4news.4anything.com

This site provides links to regional newspapers (*Chicago Tribune* and *New York Daily News*), national news (CNN Interactive and ABC News), and international news (BBC News, the *Times of*

London, and Canadian Newsworld) on-line in English. This is a great site for students to read and compare news from around the world.

Yahooligans! News
http://www.yahooligans.com/content/news
This site is designed especially for children and includes late-breaking news in the U.S. and throughout the world. There are links to many news sources, news magazines, and newspapers that cover such topics as science, nature, and sports news.

Teacher Resources

Calgary Herald Education Online
http://calgaryherald.com/education
This site is sponsored by the Parent Connection and includes teaching units designed by the American Newspaper Association and the International Reading Association for creating a newspaper in the classroom. The teaching materials include three main sections: Section 1 includes lesson plans and objectives; Section 2 contains student worksheets; and Section 3 includes a glossary of terms associated with the field of journalism.

New York Times
http://www.nytimes.com/learning
This site is sponsored by the *New York Times* on the Web/Learning Network for grades 3–12. The *New York Times* has one of the oldest Newspaper in Education programs, and this site contains a free news service for students. This program also includes curriculum guides for teaching with the newspaper and daily lesson plans for using the newspaper in the classroom.

The Write Site
http://www.writesite.org
The Write Site is designed primarily for middle school students, although elementary teachers and students would benefit from some of the resources offered on this site. Elementary students might enjoy the tour of the newsroom. Elementary teachers can use the editors desk, which provides links to related Web sites and teaching resources for using the newspaper in the classroom. The section called Extra includes lesson plans for teaching about the newspaper and journalism.

The Writing Company
http://www.writingco.com
This site is sponsored by the Division of Social Studies School Service. It includes links to sites related to teaching journalism and the newspaper. There is also an extensive database of newspapers, videos, sample lessons, and activity books.

USA Today
http://www.usatoday.com
Based on the popular newspaper, *USA Today*, this Web site contains current and past issues of the newspaper online, as well as links for teachers, parents, and students. This page contains ideas for classroom instruction on the day's lead stories.

Print Resources for Teachers and Students

Bentley, N., Guthrie, D., & Arnsteed, K. (1998). *The Young Journalist's book: How to write and produce your own newspaper.* New York: Millbrook Press.

Cheyney, A.B. (1992). *Teaching reading skills through the newspaper.* Newark, DE: International Reading Association.

Clark, R. & Clark, P. (1995). *Free to write: A journalist teaches young writers.* Portsmouth, NH: Heinemann.

Crosby, D. (1995). *Create your own class newspaper: A complete guide for planning, writing, and publishing a newspaper.* Nashville, TN: Incentive Publishing

Garrett, S.D., McCallum, S., & Yoder, M. (1996). *Mastering the message.* Lancaster, PA: Lancaster Newspapers.

Gibbons, G. (1987). *Deadline: From news to newspaper.* New York: Ty Crowell Co.

Goldstein, N. (Ed.). (1998). *The Associated Press stylebook and libel manual.* Reading, MA: Perseus Books.

Granfield, L. (1993). *Extra! Extra! The who, what, where, when, and why of newspapers.* New York: Orchard.

Leedy, L. (1991). *Messages in the mailbox: How to write a letter.* New York: Holiday House.

Leedy, L. (1993). *The furry news: How to make a newspaper.* New York: Holiday House.

Levin, M. (1997). *Kids in print—Publishing a school newspaper.* New York: Good Apple.

Levin, M. (2000). *The reporters' notebook-writing tools for student journalists.* Columbus, NC: Mind-Stretch Publishing.

Newspaper Association of America Foundation & International Reading Association. (1999). *Press ahead! A teacher's guide to creating student newspapers.* Vienna, VA & Newark, DE: Authors.

Olivares, R.A. (1993). *Using the newspaper to teach ESL learners.* Newark, DE: International Reading Association.

Strunk, W., White, E.B., Osgood, C. (1999). *The elements of style.* Boston: Allyn & Bacon.

References

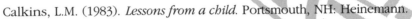

Calkins, L.M. (1983). *Lessons from a child.* Portsmouth, NH: Heinemann.

Dahl, K., & Farnan, N. (1998). *Children's writing: Perspectives from research.* Newark, DE: International Reading Association; Chicago: National Reading Conference.

Denman, L. (1995). Writers, editors, and readers: Authentic assessment in newspaper class. *English Journal, 84*(7), 55–57.

Graves, D.H. (1994). *A fresh look at writing.* Portsmouth, NH: Heinemann.

Heller, M.F. (1995). *Reading–writing connections: From theory to practice.* White Plains, NY: Longman.

Olivares, R. (1993). *Using the newspaper to teach ESL learners.* Newark, DE: International Reading Association.

Pappas, C.C., Kiefer, B.Z., & Levstik, L.S. (1995). *An integrated language perspective in the elementary school—Theory into practice.* White Plains, NY: Longman.

Shanahan, T. (1997). Reading-writing relationships, thematic units, inquiry learning...In pursuit of effective integrated literacy instruction. *The Reading Teacher, 51*(1), 12–19.

Short, K.G., Harste, J.C., with Burke, C. (1996). *Creating classrooms for authors and inquirers.* Portsmouth, NH: Heinemann.

Steelman, J.D. (1991). *Writing achievement of middle level students using computers to write a newspaper.* Eric Document Reproduction Service No. (ED 332 205).

Tompkins, G.E. (1994). *Teaching writing: Balancing process and product.* Englewood Cliffs, NJ: Macmillan.

Tonjes, M., Wolpow, R., & Zintz, N. (1999). *Integrated content literacy* (4th ed.). Boston: McGraw-Hill.